# Stankevich and His Moscow Circle
## 1830–1840

# STANKEVICH
# AND HIS MOSCOW CIRCLE
# 1830-1840

Edward J. Brown

1966

STANFORD UNIVERSITY PRESS

STANFORD CALIFORNIA

# Acknowledgments

This book reached its present form through a long process of research and writing. A generous grant from the Howard Foundation, which is administered by Brown University, enabled me to begin work in the fall of 1955. The Social Science Research Council assisted in the acquisition of important materials. The Inter-University Committee on Travel Grants underwrote trips during two summers—1956 and 1957—to the Soviet Union, where access was gained to important unpublished archives. Support came from Brown University in the form of summer research stipends in 1960 and 1961. A final research grant from Indiana University for the summer of 1965 saw the work through to its completion.

The author is in great debt not only to the institutions mentioned above, but to many individuals who gave time and attention to the manuscript and made valuable suggestions for its improvement. Among these are Sir Isaiah Berlin, of All Souls' College, Oxford; Professor Hugh McLean, Chairman of the Department of Slavic Languages at the University of Chicago; and Professor Leopold Haimson, of Columbia University. Special gratitude is due to Barnaby C. Keeney, President of Brown University, for his unfailing support and encouragement over many years. And a unique debt is owed my wife, who endured and aided magnificently.

E. J. B.

March 1966

# Contents

# Stankevich and His Moscow Circle
## 1830–1840

# Introduction

This is not a conventional biography, although the main facts in the life of its subject are given as an essential framework. Nor is it primarily a study of intellectual history, though it deals with a group of young men, the "Stankevich circle," who were the forerunners of the Russian intelligentsia of later times. It is not offered as literary criticism, though it analyzes the literary tastes and opinions of these young men and, to some extent, their published writings. It may perhaps be called an experiment in biography, since it examines the members of the Moscow circle who provided the evidence upon which a biographical study would have to be based. What has been attempted is not so much a portrayal of a famous historical personality as a study of the processes by which the history of a life or of a period grows into a significant story. For history, as we receive it, tends to have the qualities of good narrative fiction—it exhibits, that is, both content and form. The raw and untreated truth we seldom perceive. Rather, the past is a collective esthetic product, fashioned and refashioned according to the needs and hopes of many generations.

"Poetry," said Aristotle, "is a more philosophical and a higher thing than history: for poetry tends to express the universal, history the particular." Those who fashioned the history of Stankevich were unconsciously striving for poetry in Aristotle's meaning of the term, and the narrative they worked out had in it beauty, tragedy, and universal significance. My critical study of that narrative, undertaken more than a century after it took form, inevitably developed into an investigation of its artificers, and each evidential footnote was cross-examined in turn. The result is a biography on three levels: a search for the "real" Stankevich; an examination of the idealized image preserved by his posterity; and an account of the activities of the circle as a whole, outlining the intellectual concerns and motives of the men who preserved that image. The circle, moreover, is interesting in itself because it represents a kind of infancy of the Russian intelligentsia. In their literary and philosophical discussions, these young men raised nearly all the problems that were to agitate the Russian intellectual world during the nineteenth century, but these problems were still in embryonic form, and lines of thought, each of which later developed a distinct character, were as yet undifferentiated.

A biographer becomes aware that a sense of uncertainty must temper his evaluation of sources. Memory is faulty, documents may be misleading, letters and diaries are selectively preserved and full of ulterior purpose, historians are poets at heart; and if the subject was himself an avowed poet, the works he wrote will be interesting for their linguistic and intellectual quality, but may have little relevance to the facts of history or of his own life. The biographer himself, moreover, a local and particular intelligence observing the elusive atoms of recorded history, may unconsciously alter their arrangement in accordance with the structure of his own *Zeitgeist*. Uncertainty, therefore, is the essence of the matter. Croce put this very well: "The practical need that is at the basis of every historical judgment gives all history the character of 'contemporary history,' because though the facts are remote, or very remote, history always has reference to present need and to the present situation in which those facts propagate their vibrations." We shall see that of the historians who have addressed themselves to Stankevich, including the "primary sources" who knew him in the flesh, each has resonated in his own way to the man and to his period. Old interpretations are modified or abandoned when they are no longer relevant to contemporary interests and concerns.

This study lays claim to as much objectivity as may be possible in historical writing. Only verified items are reported as facts. An attempt has been made to discover Stankevich as a historical person, and to estimate his significance in Russian intellectual history. And in the course of our search for Stankevich we will make the acquaintance of a number of fascinating human beings who knew and revered him—romantic poets and government officials, Maecenases, literary critics, and sensitive ladies.

# I

# The Man and the Setting

In Moscow during the 1830's there was a group of young intellectuals who played a role of the first importance in the development of Russian thought and Russian literature. The Stankevich circle, as the group was called, included a number of outstanding writers and critics. One of its members was Vissarion Belinsky, perhaps the most influential Russian literary critic of the nineteenth century. It included the novelist Ivan Turgenev, as well as the future leader of European anarchism, Mikhail Bakunin. The center, the soul, and the conscience of the circle was Nikolai Stankevich, who, after his death in 1840 at the age of 27, became for his friends an object of worshipful devotion.

## The Image of Stankevich

The circle was a loosely organized intellectual fraternity with literary and philosophical interests. Its members met irregularly to read romantic literature—their own and others'—to discuss ideas, and to explore the philosophy of Schelling, Kant, Fichte, and Hegel. They were all at that time devotees of Western thought and culture, and they looked upon a mastery of German philosophy as a necessary attainment of the free mind.

But the atmosphere of Moscow was heavy with fear and oppression in the 1830's. Landowners and uniformed officials, who set the tone of the times, regarded philosophy with contempt or suspicion, and the great mass of Russians was apathetic and illiterate. The members of the Stankevich circle, lacking the support of a cultivated society, alone in an environment that was hostile or indifferent, thought of themselves as chosen to keep alive the pure light of learning. Such a situation provided fertile ground for the cultivation of romantic myths, and the center of the circle, Stankevich, after his death grew into a legendary, albeit rather misty, figure.

Stankevich's friends of the circle honored him as an ideal human being, for whose very existence they were grateful. They describe him as a young man of powerful and original mind who was at the same time gentle in mien, chaste in spirit, and utterly selfless. When disease took him away from them at an early age, their shock and pain at the loss of this extraordinary human being was almost too great to be borne. Belinsky felt a dull pain "heavier than grief." The historian Timofei Granovsky said that it was impossible to believe in the loss: "It is terrible to think of his death. My heart refuses to believe. ... In him I have lost the better half of myself." It was some time before they could accept the simple fact that Stankevich was dead—irreparably, finally, irrevocably dead. Bakunin was so desolated that though he had abandoned traditional religious faith, he now sought some philosophical ground for believing in personal immortality. Bakunin's sister Varvara, who was with Stankevich when he died, tried to comfort herself with the notion of a kind of pantheistic immortality through the return of the individual, separate existence into the general life of nature. And yet she could find no real consolation in the thought that Stankevich was immortal only in the sense that he was now joined with the whole of existence: such an immortality seemed to her nothing but—death. Belinsky, a rebellious young man who was never on easy terms with the universe, refused to accept tamely the senseless destruction in death of that "great spirit," and he wrote a ringing indictment of the Universal Mind: "What is this Absolute, a Moloch that eats up its own creatures, a Saturn that devours its own children? Why was Stankevich born, and why did he live? What is left of that life?" And these sentiments of his immediate friends found an echo many years later in the comments of a man who had never known Stankevich, but had merely read his biography and correspondence, Leo Tolstoy:

I've never loved anyone as I love that man, whom I've never met. What purity! What tenderness! ... And such a man suffered all his life and died in pain, while others enjoy good health and are quite complacent. Just try after that to judge between good and evil.[1]

The death of Stankevich led his friends, all of whom had been Hegelian in their orientation, to question the rational nature of the universe and to speak of the universal "Mind" in terms of revulsion or despair. There is a presentiment in these comments of that sense of the "absurd" in human life which at about the same time led Kierkegaard away from Hegel, and which is to be found in much recent literature and philosophy.

## A Brief Life

Stankevich, whether or not he was himself a philosopher, was clearly the cause of philosophical reflections in others. This is all the more remarkable because in his short life he accomplished nothing, and wrote nothing of interest except his brilliant and heretofore neglected correspondence. A sketch of his life and activities, one confined to verifiable facts, should perhaps precede our investigation of his relationship to the circle. He was born in 1813, in the village of Uderevka, in the Ostrogozhsk district of Voronezh province. His father owned the "village," a landed estate including some thousands of enserfed "souls." His family was both noble and wealthy, and his childhood, his biographers tell us, was "happy and carefree." They also tell us that he very early exhibited symptoms of the tuberculosis which brought on his death. They recount something about his life as a boy and an adolescent, and though their works are colored by reverence for a rare human, they do agree on a number of factual details, some important and some not. At the age of five, for instance, he set fire to an old house in his father's village by exploding a hunting weapon in the direction of its thatched roof—a "trick" which is taken as evidence of a certain liveliness and unpredictability. When he was ten, his father, a man who tried to put into practice his democratic principles, sent him to the Ostrogozhsk district school; there, although he was the son of a local grandee, he was tutored in common with the sons of officials, artisans, merchants, and the like. Such an educational experience was rare among the children of the provincial nobility. The elder Stankevich carried his egalitarianism to the point of having his sons and the serf boys their age treated as equals in his home. It may have been as a result of this early training that Stankevich, as a student in Moscow, showed such strong inclination toward men of plebeian origin: Belinsky, Aleksey Koltsov, Neverov, and many others.

At the age of twelve, in 1825, Stankevich was transferred to the Voronezh school for the sons of the nobility (*blagorodny pansion*), where he began his preparation for the university. Little is known of his experiences at the Voronezh school, but it is certain that he was brilliantly prepared in both language and literature. He learned to read and speak German and French reasonably well, and he developed very early a strong bias in favor of German literature. His literary skills developed so rapidly that in his first year at the university he wrote and published a patriotic verse play in the style of Schiller. Toward the end of his stay in Voronezh, in 1830, Stankevich made the acquaintance of Aleksey Koltsov, a cattle dealer and self-taught poet whose work impressed him so much that he sent some of Koltsov's poems to the *Literary Gazette,* where they were published the following year.

In the late summer of 1830 Stankevich moved to Moscow, where he was admitted to the university as a student in the literature section. There he lived in the home of Professor M. G. Pavlov, who, though his official specialties were listed as "physics, mineralogy, and agriculture," was an energetic proponent of Schelling's Naturphilosophie. Frequent converse with Pavlov, social connections with the romantic idealist N. A. Melgunov, and attendance at the lectures of Professor N. I. Nadezhdin provided Stankevich with an introduction to the German idealistic philosophers, whose doctrines, though only vaguely understood, were widely held by Russian intellectuals of the day. Until 1836, these ideas were dominant in the Stankevich circle. The idiom of the German romantics was the common possession of all the circle's members, but Stankevich was the first one of them who felt it necessary to make a systematic study of Schelling, Kant, and then Hegel.

In Moscow Stankevich studied music under the German composer F. K. Gebel; he became an accomplished pianist, and music is one of the chief topics in his epistolary essays. Poetry also concerned him during his university days, and he was a frequent contributor to the literary magazines. Philosophy and history, however, were to become his principal interests. In the course of his university career he found time to produce a dissertation, "On the Causes of the Gradual Rise of Moscow to Preeminence during the Period up to the Death of Ivan III," and to translate articles on philosophy from French reviews.

The circle known by Stankevich's name was the most important of the many circles which took form at Moscow University in the 1830's. It was a casually organized body which met on Fridays in Stankevich's quarters to discuss philosophy, listen to music, and read romantic poetry. One member of the circle, the Slavophile and poet Konstantin Aksakov, has left us a vivid description of a typical gathering: "If you dropped in at those low-ceilinged rooms full of tobacco smoke you would witness a lively and variegated scene: the piano playing, the sound of voices singing, young and gay faces on all sides, and at the piano a handsome young man whose dark, almost black locks covered his temples. Bright, intelligent eyes lit up his face."

The membership of the circle varied from year to year, as some left the University and Moscow and others replaced them. The earliest members were Yanuarii Neverov, Stankevich's closest friend, who became a government official; Ivan Kliushnikov and Vasilii Krasov, both distinguished minor poets; Yakov Pocheka, who was also a member of Herzen's circle; Sergei Stroev, a historian and paleographer; and Ivan Obolensky. In 1833 Neverov received his degree and left for St. Petersburg, but in the same year the circle acquired new members: Vissarion Belinsky and Konstantin Aksakov, Osip Bodyansky and Pavel Petrov (both of whom became famous philologists), Alexander Efremov and Alexander Keller. Stankevich received his degree in 1834. Until 1837 he spent part of each year in Moscow, and the circle continued to function, adding important new members: Mikhail Bakunin, Timofei Granovsky, and Mikhail Katkov, a vigorous young man who later became famous as a conservative literary theorist and publisher. Among those associated with the circle, though not as regular members, we should mention Stankevich's discovery, the poet A. V. Koltsov; a friend, Alexei Beyer; the young ladies of the

Beyer family, Natalie and Alexandra; and the sisters of Bakunin—Varvara, Tatiana, and Liuba. These young women frequently added to the discussion of romantic philosophy the stimulus of feminine intelligence. At the end of the decade, the novelist Turgenev became a member of the circle and a devoted follower of Stankevich.

Even after Stankevich left for Berlin in 1837 the circle continued to exist. Bakunin and Belinsky were its dominant figures for the next two years, but there was continual discord between them. When Belinsky departed for St. Petersburg in 1839 and Bakunin for Germany in 1840, the circle as such ceased to exist.

After graduating with high honors from the University in the summer of 1834, Stankevich visited briefly in St. Petersburg; then in October 1834 he returned to his native village, where he was appointed "honorary inspector of schools" for Ostrogozhsk. The appointment, with its attendant uniform and dignities, he treated with gentle mockery in his letters, though he did take his position seriously enough to formulate a number of radical ideas and plans: the introduction of the Lancastrian method of mutual instruction, the abolition of corporal punishment, and the establishment of a relationship of mutual respect between students and teachers. There is no evidence that in the short time at his disposal he tried to put any of these plans into effect. He was released from his duties as "honorary inspector" when he left for Germany in 1837.

Stankevich suffered from tuberculosis. The first reference to serious trouble occurred in letters to Neverov written in 1833, and from then on, recurrent fever and harsh coughing with issue of blood were mentioned with alarming regularity in the correspondence. It is distressing to read of the treatments prescribed at various times by his doctors—measures which may have hastened the progress of the disease. He left Russia on the long journey to Berlin and Rome at their advice. For Stankevich himself, however, the principal purpose of the trip was to study philosophy in Berlin. There he studied privately with the Hegelian philosopher, poet, and minor dramatist, Karl Werder, and read voraciously in philosophy and history. He was a frequent visitor at the Russian salon maintained in Berlin by the

Frolovs, where he met many prominent figures from the world of German literature and philosophy, including Bettina von Arnim. His health continued to grow worse. He traveled to Salzbrunn, then to Italy, where in April 1840 the disease took a fatal turn. In May his doctors advised him to spend the summer at Lake Como. He died on the way, June 24, 1840, in the town of Novi Ligure, about forty miles north of Genoa on the road to Milan.

It is clear enough that his brief life was poor in accomplishment. The history of his intellectual development, however, would have been interesting, had he written it. He began as a romantic poet and philosopher, but early discovered in himself an insistent urge toward clear, systematic, and sharply contoured thought. In place of hazy, romantic abstractions, he looked for reality and pragmatic tests. Those who describe him simply as a romantic, citing his earliest letters and his poetry, overlook the fact that in Germany he studied not only Hegel and history, but also agriculture and manufacturing. He was a romantic who was developing practical interests, and an exceptionally clearheaded student and expositor of German philosophy.

## The Importance of Circles

The Stankevich circle was the source of the idea that its leader was a historical figure of transcendent importance; and if we are to examine and assess that idea, we must first attempt to understand why circles themselves were so important to Russian intellectuals of the early nineteenth century.

A special effort of the imagination is required to understand how Russian life and literature appeared to intellectuals who were coming of age in the 1830's. For them the prospect was desolate, though not devoid of hope. In 1835 it may well have appeared to them that, as Belinsky said, there was no Russian literature. The names of a number of gifted poets might have been cited to confute him; yet Belinsky's further contention that a few names "do not constitute a literature" carried conviction to the men of his generation. What we think of today as Russian literature did not exist for them. Lermontov had not begun to publish; Gogol's collections of stories *Mirgorod* and *Ara-*

*beski* had just appeared; Pushkin seemed a fading light, and his real significance would not become known until after his death; and Turgenev, Dostoevsky, and Tolstoy had not yet come of age. Marlinsky's romantic adventure stories were the sort of thing that gained popularity. Russian literature, if indeed one could speak of such a thing, seemed the product of a few facile imitators of various European literary styles.

The intellectual poverty of the era is suggested by the state of the literary magazines. The publications open to aspiring writers were few, slight, and ephemeral; they reached a reading public of only a few hundred subscribers in all of Russia and died easily of inanition or through government action. In order to attract subscribers, editors of serious magazines were obliged to include various "miscellanies," or to print supplements containing fashion notes, Parisian anecdote and rumor, occasional verse, and other idle bits of journalism. Two independent journalistic enterprises of the thirties—perhaps the most substantial and serious of the lot—were closed by imperial fiat because of suspected anti-government leanings. One of these, *The Telescope,* was the chief outlet for the literary efforts of Stankevich and his circle. The state of the literary journals reveals the isolation of the Moscow intellectuals, and explains the importance to them of the "circle," where ideas could be advanced and discussed, and an audience found for poems, plays, and stories.[2] Between the years 1830 and 1835, ten periodical publications were initiated to accommodate, among other things, belles lettres and literary criticism; but only one of these, the *Biblioteka dlya chteniya (Library for Reading)* survived into the forties. And the exception is itself significant: the *Library for Reading* was a conservative organ, and its literary policies were repellent to the young men of the circle. "Senkovsky is a knave and his *Library* is a filthy thing," Belinsky pontificated in a letter to a friend.

Cultural stagnation was the persistent theme of a number of writers who caught the attention of the young men who formed the circle. Professor Nikolai Nadezhdin, who had a profound influence both through his lectures at Moscow University and through articles in his journal, *The Telescope,* regularly called attention in stilted prose to "the absence of bloom" in Russian letters; Ivan Kireevsky, who later became a leader of the Slavophile movement, maintained in his journal, *The European,* that Russia, having as yet no culture of its own, must first assimilate the culture of the West; Chaadaev's "Philosophical Letter," publication of which led to the suppression of *The Telescope,* offered a theory of Russian history which is in general agreement with that of Kireevsky, but expressed in the accents of gloomy satire.[3] And the young critic Belinsky, who was in a sense a product of the circle, made his literary debut with an article entitled "Literary Musings," in which his main thesis was that Russia had no literature, though he preached also the optimistic tidings of an original, native, and national Russian literature that would surely develop.[4]

The men who formed the Stankevich circle regarded Russian literature and contemporary Russian culture without enthusiasm, and in their private discussions they freely expressed dissatisfaction with both. When Belinsky, a young university expellee fond of twitting his elders, published his irreverent attack on the current literary demigods he was giving vent to ideas and feelings shared by his comrades; and when conservative writers fell upon him with patriotic scorn, he received warm support from the circle. The appearance in 1834 of Belinsky's first articles caused a wide rift to develop between the young intellectuals of the circle and the defenders of tradition in the literary field. This may have been the origin of that sense of apartness and special mission experienced by the Russian intelligentsia throughout the nineteenth century.

Though most of the members of the Stankevich circle were interested in philosophy rather than in politics or social thought, and though they seem to have looked with distrust on political radicals, recently published archives of the Czarist police bear witness to the fact that they, too, suffered from the atmosphere of oppression.[5] Suspicion fell upon any group interested in "foreign" philosophies or in recondite discussions of any kind. Isolated in an ignorant and hostile environment, these young men naturally drew closer to one another. The circle became a close-knit, exclusive group providing for its members the intellectual stimulation that could not be found elsewhere. It also provided comradeship, community of interest, and collective support in all one's affairs. The member of the circle was alone in no department of his life. His fellows took an active interest in his intellectual development, and in his moral, physical, and financial condition; and if he had tasks to perform they would often help him "as a group."[6] They interested themselves in one another's love affairs, determined as they were to keep these on the highest level of romantic experience—ideally, a kind of philosophical monasticism à deux.

Stankevich wrote one short story, "A Few Moments in the Life of Count Z.," in which the autobiographical main character, moved by a holy urge to seek truth, traveled to Moscow in order to find comrades who would help him in his search, and to "enter with them into a union of brotherhood." Count Z. felt only contempt for, and alienation from, "the crowd"—that is to say, all of those not consecrated in the holy brotherhood. In this story Stankevich expressed the sense of special vocation that held together the members of his circle.[7] And the novelist Turgenev, who belonged both to the Stankevich circle and to the group that later formed around Belinsky, has given us a vivid statement of the function of the circle in the life of a sensitive young intellectual:

When you look about you, you see that bribery flourishes; serfdom stands as firm as a rock; the military barracks are in the foreground of life; justice is nowhere to be found; . . . trips abroad have become impossible; it is impossible even to order a decent book from abroad; a kind of dark cloud hangs over all of the so-called scholarly and literary authorities; . . . Among the youth there are neither common ties nor common interests; "to the devil with them!" you say. They are all debased with fear. But then you repair to Belinsky's apartment, a second and a third friend arrive, a conversation starts—and you suddenly feel much better.[8]

For Turgenev, the circle was much more than a gathering of intellectual companions. It was an oasis of honesty offering a respite from fear, and a recreation from banality. For him, Stankevich diffused a special aura of purity and idealism.

## The Romantic Philosophy

In the early thirties the Stankevich circle was a belated and peripheral reflection of the European romantic movement. The term "romantic,"

so difficult to define and apply, is the only one that properly generalizes
the complex of attitudes which the members cultivated. They were
disaffiliated from established ideology and official doctrine in literature and philosophy, as well as in other things. They had a deep sense
of Russia's cultural backwardness, but they actively shared the faith
of Belinsky that the seeds of greatness lay buried in the Russian folk
and would soon spring up in a rich and autonomous growth of literature and art. Romantic philosophy, chiefly the ideas of Herder and
Schelling, provided support for their faith in Russia. Of the many
varieties of romanticism, the one that was most significant in Russian
intellectual life was the romanticism of nationality—the search for
native and natural genius. In an exact historical sense, even the extreme doctrines that later took form in Russian Slavophile circles
were a German importation. If we are to understand Stankevich, we
must examine first the intellectual soil which produced him and his
circle.

German romanticism had been established in Russia as an intellectual fashion by the so-called "wisdom lovers" of the eighteen twenties,
who had rejected the rationalism of the French and English schools
and propagated the ideas of Schelling. German philosophy reached
the generation of the thirties as a set of notions derived from the
thought of Schelling, Schiller, and their German followers. After
1836 certain ideas of Fichte and Hegel were intermixed with these to
form a conglomerate mass. A haze of idealistic "wisdom" suffused the
atmosphere of the day and affected the thinking of most intellectuals,
even though, with few exceptions, they had no direct knowledge of
any German sources.[9]

The vague idealism of the thirties may be reduced without excessive
schematism to three main tenets. (1) The concern of knowledge is
not with disparate empirical facts, "the coarse immediacy of matter,"
but with a unitary concept of the world as a whole. (2) The human
consciousness penetrates into the essence of things through the experience of artistic creation. (3) History is the development of humanity as a whole, and each nation is called upon to express some
single aspect of the life of all mankind. We shall examine these three
tenets in turn.

A clear and compendious statement of the wisdom the Stankevich circle inherited from its forebears, the "wisdom lovers" of the twenties, is a manuscript written by Stankevich himself in 1833, before he had read Schelling. It is in the form of a philosophic missive to his friend Neverov, and bears the title "My Metaphysics." In it Stankevich sets forth succinctly his idea of the universe as a unitary product of reason:

The knowledge which we have from our senses assures us that an external nature [the universe] does exist. Nature is a single whole composed of many separate things. The life of nature moves within the separate things, but independently of them and almost always without their being conscious of it, and always without their participation, obeying its own laws, which are eternal. . . . Although the separate things are not conscious of themselves, the life that is distributed among all these individual things must be conscious of itself since its movements have purpose. Thus life as a whole is consciousness.

The various species of things make up an ascending ladder through which life, conscious of itself as a whole, moves toward self-realization in individuals. . . . In the case of man this universal life has at last become aware of itself in a separate individual creation. Thus man is not lost in the infinity of the universe . . . but in exactly the same way that nature is conscious of itself as a whole, he is conscious of himself as a separate entity. And therefore man is able to feel an identity between himself and the world reason, he can penetrate its laws, foresee its purposes and experience the beauty of creation. In this sense man is an image of the creator (the world reason).[10]

Here we find neatly expressed the Schellingian notion of a synchronic rather than diachronic evolutionary system, of a "chain of being" in which each minuscule item of existence has its necessary place; a chain that leads onward and upward to the human intelligence and the consciousness of divinity.

The esthetic theories of Schiller and Schelling provided the idealists of the Stankevich circle with the concept of art as the summit of philosophy and the quintessential key to the "beauty of creation." "The objective world," wrote Schelling, "is only the original, still-unconscious poetry of the soul. The universal organum of philosophy —the keystone of its entire arch—is the philosophy of art." Artistic creation, for the generation of Stankevich, was neither play nor work —it was not reducible to terms of either pleasure or profit; it was as far from utilitarian preachment as from verbal or formal play. For them the activity of the artist was the highest point of philosophic—and therefore of human—activity.

The third widely held tenet—that each nation was somehow destined to make an individual contribution to human culture, adding the product of its peculiar genius to the world of art—seemed to the men of the thirties a promise that Russia would not, as Chaadaev had feared, be left out of history, but would inevitably grow to greatness in philosophy, literature, and art. To those who entertained this philosophy, the dismal state of Russian literature in the eighteen thirties might even have seemed a cause for hope: because Russia had as yet produced nothing original, her future greatness was assured. An extreme statement of this position was made by the young Belinsky, who, when he reflected on the imitative nature of Russian literature, maintained that it was the peculiar destiny of Russia, having assimilated the experience of all races and nations, to sum up this experience in great works of art. Further than this no one could go; and many years later Dostoevsky, in his famous speech on the significance of Pushkin for world literature, appropriated this idea from Belinsky, his old ideological adversary.[11]

The strength and persistence of the romantic philosophy of nationality is explained in part by the fact that the Russian intellectuals found in it a complex of doctrines which gave them comfort in their poverty. Under the spell of these doctrines, they looked for signs of a "national" literature. They listened for the sound of authentic Russian voices: and they discovered Gogol, then Lermontov. They looked for young men of lowly origin who would provide evidence of the talent buried in the folk: and there soon emerged Belinsky, the "plebeian" critic, and Koltsov, the "peasant" poet. They searched among themselves for heroic personalities whose influence would be salutary and whose memory would forever serve as inspiration and example: that is how they found—or created—Stankevich.

To present a "true" account of Stankevich and his Moscow circle is not easy task. The contemporaries of Stankevich tend to describe the events and personalities of their day in exalted terms, and historians have thus been obliged to draw their information from sources which, though primary, are suspect. The rigors of Czarist censorship, moreover, made it impossible until about fifteen years after the death of Stankevich to discuss his era in print, and during that time romantic legends grew in the dark. Russians of a later day, even positivists and scientific rationalists, tended to accept without criticism patterns that had already been worked into the fabric of history.

We shall examine the evidence upon which our knowledge of the Stankevich circle is based, paying close attention to the character and concerns of the men who produced it. Much of this evidence is direct and primary: the published works of Stankevich himself; the reminiscences, both published and unpublished, of men who knew him in Moscow or Berlin; biographies, both published and unpublished; and Stankevich's voluminous correspondence. From this study there will emerge two distinct personalities: the sainted paragon of wisdom and virtue created by Stankevich's posterity, and the man himself, an interesting and attractive young student, perplexed in love and groping for philosophy, who wrote honest, intelligent, and occasionally humorous commentaries on both topics. The examination of this evidence will reveal the process by which a romantic legend was created, and the complex needs it satisfied.

# 2

# Stankevich and His Friends

Stankevich's literary work was neither distinguished nor widely known. When he began to write in 1831 literary publishing in Russia was not a thriving field, and the magazine in which his first work appeared was slight and trivial. His earliest poems, and excerpts from his drama *Vasily Shuisky,* appeared in *Babochka* (*The Butterfly*), a journalistic miscellany featuring a bright and frothy cosmopolitanism. In each issue, along with humorous anecdotes, a haphazard potpourri of news from foreign capitals, fashion notes, brief literary reviews, bright epigrams, travelogs, and the like, a few lyric poems were included, for some of which Stankevich was responsible.

In 1831 some of his poems appeared in the *Literary Gazette,* in which Pushkin and Gogol had also published; but this promising literary venture had trouble with the Czarist censors, and came to an end less than two years after the first issue. The greater part of Stankevich's literary production appeared in *The Telescope* and its supplement *Molva* (*Rumor*), which were published in Moscow from 1831 to 1836. The editor of these journals, Professor Nadezhdin, drew upon the talent of the younger generation, and for a time the Stankevich circle undertook a kind of collective responsibility for these publications.[1]

### The Young Versifier

Stankevich's few published works suggest that he is a young and unformed litterateur, consciously imitating the German romantics but singularly inept in his efforts to reduce their themes and moods to

Russian poetry. The democratic élan of Schiller's drama finds only a pale reflection in the tragedy *Vasily Shuisky,* which Stankevich published at nineteen. When the complete work appeared in book form Stankevich, feeling the full horror of what he had done, bought up all the copies he could find and destroyed them, thus adding one more item to the list of Russian bibliographical rarities.[2] A patriotic feeling for the Russian people, praise of freedom and the democratic spirit, and pictures of heroism and self-sacrifice are all present in the play, but the blank-verse iambic pentameters lack both the imagery and the rhythmic power to convey these things effectively. Indeed, the poems of this young romantic show a curious deafness to rhythm; and poetic images give way to abstract statements of ideas current in the plays and historical novels of the day. His first literary effort is clear evidence that Stankevich, though he may have been a philosopher, was certainly not a poet.

His few dozen poorly turned lyrics—which, in addition to a tragedy and one short story, constitute Stankevich's total literary production— not only have had no influence in Russian literature, they hardly have a place in it. Stankevich himself soon came to understand that his talents were in no sense literary, and he deprecated these early efforts. If we give some attention to his lyric poems here, it is because they contain important clues to the nature of his personality and influence.

Taken as a whole these poems express a kind of perplexity of spirit between the alternatives of chaste isolation within the self and involvement in "the world" and the concerns of other men. Some of them display regular alternation between hope and despair, and as a consequence of this dichotomy one line of a poem will often seem to answer another. At times hope—itself in the guise of despair—is offered only in the escape from all visible worlds into death, "which alone speaks truth." There are "Two Paths," the path of joy and the path of sorrow, and perhaps only the latter leads to heaven. There are "Two Ways of Life"—the title of a love poem that expresses the perplexing alternatives offered by the creature he kisses and the one to whom he addresses a fervent prayer. "Life's Exploit," one of the best in idea and execution, finds the ultimate reward for renunciation of the trifling pleasures of this world, not in isolation or death but in "overstepping the earthly bounds, becoming part of the universal life, which, filling you, is filled with you, through love." This poem urging renunciation of the world in the name of a higher love is Stankevich's most characteristic lyric, and perhaps it comes nearest to expressing that quality of his nature which appealed to the imagination of his contemporaries. And when "The Angel of Pleasure" diverts the poet from his true mission, he speaks to her of that other and higher love, the love which links him with the life of nature and ultimately with the thought of the creator, the love which she, weak maiden that she is, "cannot know." "The arms of my soul," says the nineteen-year-old anchorite of universal love, "contain too much in their embrace."

The main themes of Stankevich's poems were furnished by the romantic idealism which was the intellectual style of his time. His poems have their share of dreamy mysticism, pantheistic sensations, and flights of religious emotion, and they express a striving for communion with an ideal existence beyond the vulgar accidents of time and space. There are in them, however, qualities peculiar to Stankevich. Curiously enough, thought is stronger in them than feeling, and this in spite of constant emphasis on the primacy of feeling. His poetry conveys concepts rather than images, and in language that lacks poetic rhythm. His are not romantic poems at all, but philosophical meditations in the romantic manner, composed by a young man who has adopted a literary fashion but is not at home in it. Their most characteristic theme is the religious one of renunciation; there is not a scintilla of romantic rebellion in any of them. It is a paradox that they should have been written by the intellectual leader—if that is what he was—of a circle that included Belinsky and Bakunin, and from which emerged the liberal movement of the forties. Contemporaries who knew Stankevich only through his poems could not have supposed that the young man had any special significance. And his only published prose, a febrile daydream on the subject of early and untimely death "through excess of love and life," is devoid of literary merit and deservedly forgotten.[3]

## Reminiscences

The "real" Stankevich was known only to a small circle of friends. This group, however, included some of the most influential intellectual figures of the nineteenth century, and all of them paid homage to him as a leading spirit of the age. They vied with one another in extremes of adulation; they set no limits to the intellectual power and moral influence that Stankevich supposedly exercised in their midst. We have seen how Belinsky,[4] Bakunin, and Granovsky[5] reacted to his untimely death. The novelist Turgenev knew him only briefly, just before his death, but he too came under the strange spell: "He stretched out a hand to me and showed me the true path."[6]

Such statements as these, all of which appeared in private correspondence, carry the clear accent of the Russian romantic movement. The letters reveal the special value the romantics attached to friendship itself. Implicit in them is the belief in "beautiful souls" (*schöne Seele*) whose impulses are naturally good and whose influence is a spiritual therapy. Stankevich's friends saw him as one of these extraordinary beings—a "hero" not measurable by the normal scale. The letters written soon after his passing give little evidence in support of their high opinion of his powers, but they reveal much about his times and his milieu.

In the reminiscences or autobiographies of his friends, however, one would expect to find some account of what Stankevich taught them, and of what he had to say on important matters. Fellow students who knew him or claimed to have known him wrote reminiscences that touched directly on Stankevich and the circle. Among these, the most important to our inquiry were Ya. M. Neverov, K. S. Aksakov, Yakov Kostenetsky, and the novelists Goncharov and Turgenev. We shall turn now to this kind of evidence.

Yanuarii M. Neverov was one of Stankevich's most intimate and trusted friends.[7] We shall see that about a fourth of Stankevich's published correspondence consists of letters to Neverov, who preserved them as a sentimental treasure. But Neverov's *Autobiography* tells very little about Stankevich and his circle; and often what it does tell is either trivial or dubious.[8] The poverty of concrete detail concerning Stankevich in the autobiographical sketch of a man who was his "inseparable companion" is both striking and strange. Neverov does not provide the information we need to form a clear picture of Stankevich's activities, his personality, his conversation, and his effect on others. Neverov does say that he saw in him a "second Pushkin," a judgment which tells us only that Neverov's own taste in literature was uninformed. He does, however, relate an interesting anecdote about himself and the peasant poet Koltsov in which the very name of Stankevich carries the aura of heroism. At a certain party, Neverov decided to drink no more, in order to stave off disaster. Koltsov, deep in his cups, demanded that Neverov drink with him just once more. When Neverov refused. Koltsov announced that he would compel him to drink. He walked to the center of the room and, having got the attention of all the guests, delivered a speech about Stankevich which was, according to Neverov, deeply moving. Koltsov then proposed a toast to Stankevich's health, addressing himself directly to Neverov. Not to down a cup at such a solemn moment would have been an act of heresy, and Neverov records that he downed many more that night and became thoroughly drunk. The story is interesting as evidence of the reverence paid the name of Stankevich, but it reveals nothing else about him.

In the pages of Neverov's *Autobiography* Stankevich is a wraithlike figure wearing the nimbus of a "beautiful soul." In his "Reminiscences of Turgenev," Neverov recalls some opinions that Stankevich expressed, but these are utterly undistinguished and might have belonged to Neverov himself, or to many other people.[9] These recollections of Stankevich's oldest and closest friend, the man to whom, in his letters, he revealed without restraint all the secrets of his young life, are strangely uninformative and dull.

Fragmentary excerpts of Neverov's unpublished reminiscences of Stankevich have been published recently in the Soviet Union. They are from a manuscript produced in 1856 and 1857, a time when ideas of social reform occupied the minds of a growing number of people. The excerpts now published tell us little or nothing about Stankevich himself, but they bear the mark of the period of the "great reforms" and reflect widespread humanitarian concern for the liberation of the Russian serfs. We are told that Stankevich "was no stranger to thoughts concerning the civil and social organization of peoples," and that he once expressed the opinion that "the great mass of the Russian people remain in a condition of serfdom and therefore can take advantage neither of civil nor of general human rights; there is no doubt that, sooner or later, the government will remove this yoke from the people." Neverov quotes Stankevich at length on the need for general education, and he adds that Stankevich obliged his followers to take a solemn oath that they would labor for such praiseworthy aims. One must emphasize that the style of these reminiscences does not at all suggest the personality of Stankevich, whose posture was not that of one who exacts solemn promises from his friends; and their content is heavily weighted with the particular concerns of the period in which they were written. It would seem that they do not constitute important new evidence on Stankevich and his circle.[10]

Konstantin Aksakov's "Reminiscences of My Student Days, 1832–1835" were composed by a man who became one of the intellectual leaders of the Slavophile movement. He was a member of the Stankevich circle and a frequent contributor to *The Telescope* when it was edited by Belinsky in 1835. In 1855, on the occasion of the hundredth anniversary of the founding of Moscow University, he wrote the "Reminiscences."[11] They are impressionistic, conversational, and rather casual in style, perhaps because the manuscript was not at first intended for publication but was to have been read at a gathering of close friends in the home of Yurii Samarin, another ideologist of the Slavophile movement. The "Reminiscences" have a fair share of the sentimental nostalgia that might be expected when a man in middle life (one is tempted to say "a romantic in middle life") recalls his youth. Aksakov had warm memories of simple, informal conversation with his student comrades, and of the sense of equality and democratic brotherhood he experienced among them. Directness and sincerity of thought and feeling were valued then, Aksakov says, and the students who gathered at Stankevich's quarters were repelled by the false and the pretentious. Their attitude toward the national art and literature was negative. Their views were formed independently and without reference to authority—indeed, they tended to treat all authority with a certain scorn. Aksakov, a Slavophile supporter of the Czar, the Orthodox Church, and the Russian folk, claims in his memoirs to have deplored even as a youth the circle's contemptuous attitude toward the Russian state. Yet the discussions of philosophy and moral questions drew him to the circle, and he "spent every evening there."

Aksakov's reminiscences thus claim for him an intimate relation to the famous circle and its leader. But there is some reason to question what he wrote in 1855, for a recently published letter shows that in March 1837 Aksakov wrote his older brother that he had so far held himself aloof from Stankevich and his circle of friends, though he was beginning to draw closer to them.[12] In Stankevich's correspondence there is evidence of a certain suspicion and strain in his relations with Aksakov.[13] Moreover, Stankevich left Moscow in May 1837, and therefore Aksakov, if he was ever on close terms with him, could have been so only for a brief period.

These reminiscences speak only in broad generalities of Stankevich's activities and character. Aksakov remembers him as a "harmonious" spirit whose nature was as little prone to rebellion as to slavishness; for whom the institutions of church and family were sacred ("He would allow no one to attack them in his presence"); whose sane, salutary influence served as a checkrein on the extremist urges of Bakunin and Belinsky; who had bright, intelligent eyes, and (somewhat like Lensky in Pushkin's *Eugene Onegin*) dark curls that reached his shoulders. In a word, the Stankevich that existed in Aksakov's memory twenty years later strikes one suspiciously as an idealized image, and, in part at least, as a projection into the past of Aksakov's idea of himself. His remarks give no hint of Stankevich's troubled search for philosophy and love, or of the offhand, ironic humor that never failed him.

Of the regular members of the Stankevich circle, only Aksakov and Neverov wrote memoirs that dealt directly with the activities of the circle itself. The novelist Goncharov, though he attended classes with Stankevich and other members of the circle, had not known them but had only "heard" that they constituted a separate group, and that they "met and read together and exchanged opinions."[14] It is not clear whether Goncharov heard of the Stankevich circle in 1832, when he was a student in the same classes with its members, or much later, when the circle had become established in Russian intellectual history. It seems likely that the latter was the case.

Yakov Kostenetsky, who spent many years in exile because of his involvement in a seditious conspiracy to revive the Decembrist movement (the so-called "Sungurov affair"), was a classmate of Stankevich at the university. In his "Reminiscences" Kostenetsky tells of this affair, describing in grandiloquent prose his mood of romantic rebellion, as he recalled it many years later: "I was ready to become a revolutionary hero, and I dreamed not only of the triumph of success, but of the agonies of failure. I knew the history of the Decembrists and their fate did not frighten me at all. I was always ready, like them, to suffer for the great cause...."[15]

Kostenetsky claimed to have been a frequent visitor at Stankevich's apartment in the home of Professor Pavlov: "Sometimes he would read me his poems; he even read me a tragedy in verse—if I remember rightly, 'Dmitry Donskoy.' He was a very modest young man, as mild as an angel, completely devoted to learning and poetry."[16] As V. S. Nechaeva points out, Kostenetsky's memory of Stankevich may have been refreshed by the reading of Annenkov's *Biography of Stankevich,* which we will examine in the next chapter.[17] Even so, Kostenetsky had not remembered the title of Stankevich's "tragedy in verse" correctly, possibly confusing Stankevich's *Vasily Shuisky* with Belinsky's *Dmitry Kalinin.* In any case, it is doubtful that Kostenetsky was close to the circle, or that he knew Stankevich well.

Though Kostenetsky gives us no real clue to Stankevich's character and influence, yet he did manage to involve him, along with several other university friends, in his own political tragedy. After being convicted and sentenced to be shipped as a common soldier to the Caucasus, Kostenetsky addressed a letter to two Moscow friends in which he sent greetings to others whom he named, among them Neverov and Stankevich. The letter is an emotional composition in the high-flown romantic style containing references to the "sacred bond" of friendship and the "great ideals" that all the friends supposedly shared. It fell into the hands of the police, as Kostenetsky must have known it would, and a certain suspicion of guilt by association fell on all those he had named in his letter. So far as is known, none of them were actually involved in the Sungurov affair, and such a letter is not in itself evidence that they were even sympathetic to Kostenetsky's revolutionary views. In the case of Stankevich, the Czarist authorities seem to have been satisfied by a pledge he signed to have no dealings with "the former student Kostenetsky." But the emperor ordered that the students named be kept under strict surveillance. Kostenetsky's garrulous and self-conscious "Reminiscences," written when he was seventy-five, contain no reference to the episode of the letter nor to the grief he caused his "comrades."[18] Perhaps he had forgotten that.

The writers of reminiscences are often unreliable, and those who wrote about Stankevich and his circle would seem to have been exceptionally so. A physician and surgeon, N. I. Pirogov—who had no connection at all with Stankevich or his circle, but wrote of this period— has left in his "Posthumous Notes" a spontaneous and unedited impression of the mirage-like time dimension in terms of which the memoirist attempts to refigure the distant past. He wrote in his notes: "[My father died] in September 1824. That day a new era in my life began. But it's a strange thing, I'm not sure now myself that it was in 1824. There's no use looking it up now, but the strange thing is that it seems to me now my father lived much longer after I entered the university than the records show. But actually, my father died about a year before the death of Alexander I, and that happened in 1825...."[19]

### Turgenev's "Note on Stankevich" and "Rudin"

The novelist Turgenev, in his student days a devotee of German philosophy, spent his formative years immersed in the world of German romanticism. Turgenev was one of that select band of young Russians who went to Berlin as to the promised land. He was an in-

timate member of the Russian group in Europe, and was introduced
to Stankevich by Granovsky in Berlin at the end of 1838. He does not
claim to have known Stankevich well in Berlin, but became his close
friend when they met again in Rome, just a few months before Stankevich's death.[20]

Turgenev's novels contain frequent literary reflections of German
romanticism. Memories of his literary and philosophical wanderings,
suffused with nostalgic regret at the passing of youth, are a characteristic minor theme of Turgenev; there are, in his works, evocations of
the Europe he knew as a young man, and a number of characters
based on Stankevich, Bakunin, Kliushnikov, the novelist himself, or
a combination of these.

Turgenev wrote his "Note on Stankevich" in 1856 at the request of
P. V. Annenkov, who included part of it in his own biography of
Stankevich, published in 1857. The "Note" is one of very few explicit
statements about Stankevich's character and personality written by a
member of the circle itself. Though Turgenev was close to Stankevich
for only a few months, should he not have preserved a vivid image of
the man who, he said, "stretched out a hand to me and showed me the
true path"? But Turgenev's portrait is disappointing because it lacks
particular and individual contours. Other members of the Russian
community abroad who are mentioned in connection with Stankevich
stand out more clearly as real persons than does the man himself, who
has only the palest existence in Turgenev's memory. For instance,
Berta, the Berlin girl who was Stankevich's mistress and constant
companion, and whom he loved after a fashion, is a far more vivid
character than her lover (who was, Turgenev assures us, while telling
us of the days and nights Stankevich spent in her company, "chaste
in spirit").

Turgenev's recorded memories of Stankevich follow a definite pattern: he mentions an activity engaged in by Stankevich and certain
friends he visited in Rome or Berlin, then immediately focuses attention on the friends, not on Stankevich. For example, Stankevich was
fond of Berta, who said, when her sister was obliged to stay overnight
in Stankevich's apartment, that for this one night she did not believe

in *"allgemeine Pressfreiheit,"* though indeed she was a liberal. Stankevich loved the Berlin theater: his favorites were two comedians,
Hern and Beckmann, whose comic art Turgenev then briefly characterizes. Stankevich visited the Frolovs, of whom he was very fond:
Madame Frolov's Russian salon, frequented by notables from the
German world of philosophy and literature, is then described. Stankevich's remarks on Belinsky (whom Turgenev had not then met)
were friendly but amused and slightly contemptuous: Turgenev says
that he remembered one of these sallies because of Belinsky's unusual
given name, Vissarion.

What was it, finally, that drew Turgenev to Stankevich, and what
was the secret of Stankevich's influence on his followers? The following quotation from Turgenev's "Note" throws some light on this
question:

Stankevich influenced others because he never thought about himself. He
took real interest in all human beings, and, almost without being aware
of it, drew them after him into the realm of the Ideal. No one was as brilliant or as kind as he was in intellectual disputes. There wasn't a trace of
pretense in him. . . .

He was somewhat taller than average, very well built, and from his
physical appearance one would never have guessed that he was disposed
to consumption. He had fine black hair, a sloping forehead, small dark
eyes. . . . In his whole being, in all his movements, there was a kind of
graciousness, an unconscious distinction—as though he were the scion of
kingly stock but unaware of his origin.

Turgenev confesses to a sense of embarrassment, even fear, while
in Stankevich's presence, feelings suggested by the consciousness of
his own hollowness and insincerity. Other members of Stankevich's
circle professed to have felt this same sense of general unworthiness
in the man's presence. It should be noted that Turgenev emphasizes
Stankevich's distinction, making him seem a kind of fairy-tale prince
in disguise.

In the "Note on Stankevich" Turgenev states that when he described Pokorsky, a character in the novel *Rudin,* the image of Stankevich hovered before his imagination; he adds, however, that the
character of Pokorsky is only a "pale outline." But Pokorsky is no

paler than Turgenev's picture of the actual Stankevich. The "real person" eludes us in the sketch of Stankevich as it does in the characterization of Pokorsky and his circle. In *Rudin* Pokorsky does not figure in the action but is mentioned only in the reminiscences of one of the characters, whose evocation of the past stirs nostalgic regret for lost ideals and the long-cooled enthusiasm of youth. Pokorsky, the magnetic center of a circle of students devoted to the quest for truth and goodness, neither does nor says anything in the novel, but functions as the inspirer and guardian of his friends' ideals:

Having entered Pokorsky's circle, I confess to you, Alexandra Pavlovna, that I was completely transformed; I grew more humble, I inquired into things, I studied, I rejoiced, I venerated—in a word, it was as though I had entered some temple. And in very deed, as I recall our meetings, well, by God, there was much in them that was good, even moving. You imagine: some five or six lads come together, one tallow candle burning, tea of the filthiest taste is handed round, and the lumps of sugar provided with it are old, very old; but you should have seen all our faces, you should have heard our speeches! In all eyes there was rapture, and cheeks burned, and hearts beat, and we talked of God, of truth, of the future of humanity, of poetry—sometimes we talked nonsense, we were enthusiastic over trifles, but what of that? ... Pokorsky would sit with his legs tucked under him, resting his pale cheek on his hand; and his eyes would shine, would shine. Rudin would stand in the middle of the room and talk, talk eloquently, just like a young Demosthenes before a raging sea; from time to time the tousle-haired poet Subbotin would give off explosive exclamations, as if in his sleep; a forty-year-old *Bursch* named Scheller, the son of a German pastor, famous among us as the profoundest of thinkers because of his everlasting, quite inviolable silence, would be observing his silence with a special rapture; even the merry Shchitov, the Aristophanes of our meetings, would lapse into silence and only grin; two or three novitiates would be listening with exultant delight.... And the night would fly past quietly and smoothly, as though on wings. And now the dawn would be graying, and we would disperse, moved, merry, honest, sober (at that time we did not even think of wine), with a kind of pleasant weariness in our souls ... and you looked even at the stars with a kind of trustfulness, as though they had grown closer, and more intelligible.... Ah! They were great times then, and I don't like to think that they went for nothing! Nor did they, not even for those who afterwards were vulgarized by life.... How often have I happened to meet men who were my former comrades! You would

think the man had become quite an animal, but you had only to mention
the name Pokorsky in his presence and all the last remnants of nobility
within him began to stir, as though in a dark and dirty room you had
opened a forgotten phial of perfume. . . .

In his literary treatment of Stankevich there is a deliberate roman-
ticizing tendency that is absent from Turgenev's "Note on Stankevich." The poverty of the pure and dedicated youth is an invention: Stankevich was quite well off and even contributed to the support of his friends. The guttering candle and lean refreshment are
purely literary: the young men who gathered at Stankevich's apartment ate and drank well, though not usually to excess.[21]

A clue to the function of Stankevich in Turgenev's psychology is
the fact that the figure of Pokorsky in the novel serves as a foil for the
main character, Rudin. Rudin is an intellectual poser, Pokorsky a
genuine thinker. Rudin is self-conscious and theatrical, Pokorsky simple and unpretentious. Rudin is a fluent practitioner of the glittering
phrase; Pokorsky says nothing at all. Pokorsky is all the things that
Rudin—in whom there are traces of Bakunin, Herzen, Belinsky, and
Turgenev himself—is not and can never be. Pokorsky—and therefore
Stankevich—is the imagined better self of them all.[22]

In short, the reminiscences of Stankevich written by those who
knew him in Moscow and in western Europe during his student days
are worshipful but pale and uninteresting. As historical documents
they are redundant, since they add nothing to the already established
image of Stankevich as an ideal human being, an image that had
taken form among his friends soon after his death. Though written
many years later, they have not been tempered by the perspective of
time and merely echo the fervid statements to be found in the letters
of Belinsky, Bakunin, and Granovsky. The writers of these reminiscences seem to accept as fact the idealized Stankevich of the Moscow
circle, though they do not help us to see as an actual human being
that paragon of intelligence, purity, and love. Neverov, who was his
friend and counselor, Aksakov and Turgenev, who were members of
his circle, and Kostenetsky, who caused the shadow of suspicion to
fall briefly on the young man, all agree on his essential features, which

they present in an abstract and stylized composite. One is reminded
of the iconized verbal portraits in the Old Russian Chronicle, where
saints or princes are described in fixed, formulaic phrases as "fair of
face and generous to the poor," or "benevolent to their followers, full
of kindness, and with no evil in their hearts."

# 3
# Herzen and the Biographers of Stankevich

What we have learned thus far of Stankevich has been taken from the testimony of close friends who received the direct rays of his intellectual and personal charm. Many years after his death biographical sketches were published by two men who had not enjoyed the benison of his acquaintance, Alexander Herzen and P. V. Annenkov. The two agree on the significance of the Moscow circle in Russian intellectual life, and their opinion has been accepted almost without question. Subsequent generations have derived their idea of Stankevich and his circle so completely from Herzen and Annenkov that their writings deserve close and careful examination here.

## Herzen

The brilliant political writer and memoirist Herzen has been considered a prime source of information about Stankevich and his times. His autobiography, *My Past and Thoughts,* a literary achievement of the first rank, contains, in Chapter 25, a number of passages rich with memories of Moscow University in the 1830's. Herzen offers interesting and provocative commentary on professors and students, and on the intellectual life that was developing in and around the institution. Chapter 25 contains, among many other things, an essay on Stankevich and his circle, which seems to be an attempt by Herzen to convince his European friends that deep and pure wellsprings of thought and feeling moved beneath the surface of Russian life, dark and savage though that life might appear to others. Stankevich was important to Herzen as evidence that a specifically Russian cultural development could be descried even during the reign of Nicholas I.

He greeted the publication of Annenkov's *Biography and Correspondence of Stankevich* because it dealt with a native intellectual growth hitherto concealed and unrecognized. Looking back at the period between 1825 and 1855, he said,

Future generations will wonder at [its] emptiness and will search for the lost evidences of intellectual activity, which had in fact not been interrupted. To all appearances the stream had been stopped, Nicholas had tied up the artery; but the blood continued to flow in bypaths. It is precisely this capillary flow which has left its mark in the works of Belinsky, and in the correspondence of Stankevich.

Herzen, in Mirsky's happy phrase, writes with the accent of the romantic, though he is a positivist and a believer in science. The reader of *My Past and Thoughts* may be charmed by the poetic tone of the narrative, but surprised by the number of factual errors the reminiscences contain. Some of these seem at first sight to be relatively unimportant; for instance, Herzen seldom states correctly the month and year in which an event occurred. Sometimes his error involves less than a year, sometimes two or three years. These lapses in memory would not have great significance but for the fact that a very slight rearrangement of events in time often heightens the human appeal or historical significance of his narrative. This is not to suggest that Herzen is consciously fictionalizing his past; but it is a fact that his memory, by very slight shifts, sometimes rearranges events so as to lend them artistic form and a romantic aura.

One or two examples which have nothing to do with Stankevich or his circle will suffice to demonstrate Herzen's method. He asserts that when he was arrested in Moscow in 1834 he was held at first in a police station, then transferred to a dark underground cell in a prison that had once been a monastery. The transfer, he maintains, occurred after the emperor's visit to Moscow in 1834, and was the direct result of Nicholas's displeasure with the gentleness of police measures against political dissidents. Actually, he was transferred to the new quarters before the emperor's arrival in Moscow.[1] A minor slip, perhaps, yet it may be that the factual error lends the occurrence greater historical significance than the true chronology of events would have yielded.

A somewhat more deliberate mnemonic revision is involved in Herzen's account of the death of his university comrade Nebaba, whom he met again while in exile in the town of Vladimir. Nebaba was a stupid, ungainly, and physically ugly man, the object of general contempt, and he ended his life by his own hand. Herzen tells how he came upon the body of Nebaba on a street in Vladimir, outside an old church wall. He describes the corpse surrounded by a crowd of boys and tradesmen, and the police rushing to the scene. The vivid memory of the unfortunate Nebaba provides Herzen with the occasion to reflect on the cruelty of fate and the injustice of pain and suffering. The pathetic ne'er-do-well Nebaba is fixed for all time in a moving and unforgettable image. But the fact is that Nebaba killed himself only after Herzen's departure from Vladimir, and therefore Herzen could never have seen the crowd of boys, or the policemen, or the dead body of his friend.[2] These two examples of Herzen's method in *My Past and Thoughts* should indicate that acceptance of this source must be tempered with skepticism.

The passages on university life in the thirties, which tell of Stankevich and his circle, are an impressionistic mélange of characters and events interspersed with comments and bits of wisdom offered by Herzen. The borderline between the author's thought and the objective person or event that occasioned it is often blurred. It is not always easy to distinguish between Herzen and the objective facts, and the facts often gain interest in the confusion.

Though Herzen is a primary source on Stankevich and his circle, we note with some misgiving that those pages in *My Past and Thoughts* that are directly devoted to Herzen's own life at the university contain no mention of Stankevich or his associates, and there is no evidence that Herzen ever met Stankevich, or that he knew Belinsky at the university.[3]

The Stankevich circle enters into Herzen's narrative only when he tells of returning in 1840 from exile in the provinces to find that the Moscow students had a "new ideal"—that both Saint-Simon and Schelling had given place to Hegel, and that the young intellectuals of 1840 were "desperate Hegelians." Herzen describes this state of affairs in a justly famous paragraph, which deserves to be quoted if only for its literary quality:

Our young philosophers ruined not only their native language but their understanding. Their attitude toward reality became scholastic and literary. . . . Everything really direct, every simple feeling was reduced to an abstract category, and as a result became emptied of life—a pale, algebraic shadow. In all of this there was a kind of naïveté, because it was all perfectly honest. The man who went for a walk in Sokolniki went there in order to surrender himself to the pantheistic feeling of his unity with the cosmos. And if he happened to meet a tipsy soldier or a peasant woman . . . the philosopher would not simply converse with them, but "attempt to define the popular substance in an immediate and particular phenomenon."

The passage on the Hegelians is preceded in Herzen's narrative by an account of the personality and influence of his close friend and collaborator N. P. Ogaryov, who in 1840 was the attractive leader of a circle of young Hegelian intellectuals. The story of Ogaryov's life is an important episode in the history of Russian romanticism, but we are concerned here only with the image of Ogaryov that Herzen creates in Chapter 25 of *My Past and Thoughts*. This is of interest because Herzen, in his account of Stankevich, describes Stankevich's personality and influence in terms that might equally well be applied to Ogaryov.

Ogaryov, he says, was gifted with a special kind of magnetism— a feminine capacity to charm and attract. "With no apparent reason other people cling to such personalities; they are warmed, drawn closer to one another, and calmed by them. Such personalities are a free feast to which anyone may sit down in order to renew his forces, rest, become more hopeful of life. . . ." Herzen takes issue with those who accuse Ogaryov of idleness, though Ogaryov accomplished little in his life, and his published work fell far short of matching his ambitious plans for treatises on philosophy and literature, cycles of lyric poems, and works of fiction. A man of great charm and ready conversation, Ogaryov, like so many men of his generation, was utterly wanting in performance. Yet Herzen maintains that "to serve as the center of a whole circle of people is in itself a great exploit, especially in a society divided and disunited."

After describing Ogaryov, Herzen explains how German philosophy, which dominated Ogaryov's circle, was introduced into Russia. Characteristically, he finds that Pavlov, a Russian, was far more effective in his exposition of Schelling's Naturphilosophie than were the Germans themselves.* He considers it regrettable, however, that Pavlov did not submit himself to the stern discipline of Hegel's thought, but notes that Pavlov's student, Stankevich, did so with thoroughness and devotion:

Stankevich, also one of those *idle* people who accomplish *nothing,* was the first follower of Hegel in the Moscow circle. He studied German philosophy deeply and esthetically [sic]. Gifted with extraordinary talents, he was able to draw a large circle of friends into his favorite intellectual occupation. This circle was a really remarkable one, and from it came a whole phalanx of scholars, literary men and professors, among whom were Belinsky, Bakunin, and Granovsky.

Before my exile there was little sympathy between my circle and Stankevich's. We did not like their exclusively speculative interest and they did not care for our exclusively political direction. They considered us Frondists and Frenchmen, we considered them sentimentalists and Germans. The first man who was acknowledged by both of us, who offered the hand of friendship to both camps and with his warm affection and pacific nature removed the last traces of mutual misunderstanding, was Granovsky. But when I arrived in Moscow he was already in Berlin, and poor Stankevich, at the age of twenty-seven, was expiring on the shores of Lago di Como.

Sickly, mild in character, a poet and a dreamer, Stankevich was naturally more interested in contemplation and abstract thought than in purely practical questions; his artistic idealism fitted him perfectly—it was a laurel wreath resting upon the pale brow of the dying youth. Others were too healthy and had too little of the poet in them to remain long in the realm of abstract thought without making the transition to real life. An exclusively speculative interest is foreign to the Russian character, and we shall soon see that the *Russian spirit* reworked Hegelian philosophy and that *our* vital nature, in spite of all vows of philosophic monasticism, claimed its own. However, in 1840 there was as yet no thought among the young men who surrounded Ogaryov of rebelling against the letter in defense of the spirit, or against abstraction in favor of life.[4]

---

* A conclusion that reveals an important subsurface theme of *My Past and Thoughts*: the natural superiority of Russian pupils to their German teachers.

It must be said that these flowing and fascinating paragraphs have their share of inaccuracy, inconsistency, and even invention. One small point to begin with: Stankevich did not expire "on the shores of Lago di Como," but in the little town of Novi Ligure, on the road between Genoa and Milan. Moreover, since Stankevich was no longer in Moscow when Herzen returned, Herzen's notion of Stankevich's Hegelianism is at least secondhand; in fact, his knowledge of the man is derived entirely from the reports of others. And further, we shall see in a later chapter that "the transition to real life" was indeed one of Stankevich's deepest concerns.[5]

It is quite obvious that Herzen has placed Stankevich, whom he did not know, into the icon-frame belonging to the cherished friend Ogaryov, whom he knew very well. Stankevich, like Ogaryov, is accused by the philistines of idleness, in spite of his great accomplishment as the leader of a circle. He is a mild young man, "a poet and a dreamer" unsuited for "practical life" and given to "speculative thought." And we note with particular astonishment that by the end of the third paragraph Herzen has actually substituted the name of Ogaryov as the center of a Hegelian circle, though the subject of the paragraph has been Stankevich and *his* circle!

The images of Stankevich and Ogaryov are mingled, perhaps confused, in Herzen's mind. It may be that Stankevich was in reality cast in a mold like that of Ogaryov; but the evidence of Herzen's reminiscence is insufficient to bear this out. Moreover, his descriptions of both Ogaryov and Stankevich conform to a romantic stereotype already hackneyed in literature and imitated in life. The poet and dreamer, fragile and feminine in temperament, unfit for worldly care, snatched untimely from this life, is a character native to romantic literature, though indeed there do exist individuals whose lives seem to resemble this romantic pattern. It fits Herzen's comrade and collaborator, the romantic Ogaryov, in almost all particulars except the length of his life. Ogaryov died in England at the age of sixty-four after a long and happy life with Mary Sutherland, a prostitute from the streets of London, whom he had loved and saved from her fate.

Herzen's account of Stankevich's life is not wholly inconsistent with the facts, yet we see in it the typical devices of Herzen the "artist-historian": those subtle corrections of reality that give his story esthetic form. We see also the intrusion of his emotional thesis regarding the "Russian" spirit, which would always rebel against abstraction in favor of life. Moreover, his statement that Stankevich was the first follower of Hegel in the Moscow circle leaves the impression that Stankevich introduced the circle to the study of Hegel, which is not at all accurate. Before his departure for Germany Stankevich had begun to read about Hegel, and he had read Hegel's works in the original. In 1835 he undertook to translate from the French an article on Hegel which had appeared in the Parisian *Revue Germanique,* but he did not complete the translation. In 1836 he received from Neverov, who sent it to him from St. Petersburg, a complete set of Hegel's works, and references to Hegel appear thereafter with some frequency in his letters. But his departure from Moscow for Berlin in 1837 antedates by at least a year that "desperate Hegelianism" of which Herzen speaks, and it is certain that he was never its moving spirit. On the contrary, Belinsky's correspondence with Stankevich points to Bakunin and Katkov as the principal agents of his own conversion to Hegelianism. We may therefore absolve Stankevich of responsibility for this episode in the circle's intellectual development.

One possible source for Herzen's image of Stankevich in the 1854 edition of *My Past and Thoughts* is a biographical essay by N. G. Frolov, composed in 1844 but never published. Herzen had access to the manuscript of this essay and according to Granovsky had read "the first part" and expressed satisfaction with it.[6] This circumstance helps to explain Herzen's depiction of Stankevich as a sickly poet and dreamer. Frolov's biographical essay is based on selected excerpts from Stankevich's correspondence, chiefly his letters to Neverov. The earliest letters in that correspondence are concerned exclusively with romantic poetry and the varieties of subjective experience—esthetic, religious, and sentimental. Stankevich's interest in philosophy and history may not have been apparent in the portion of the essay that Herzen is said to have read.

Such is the portrait of Stankevich presented by Herzen in 1854. In the 1861 edition of *My Past and Thoughts,* Herzen filled out this rather pale stereotype with a few lively details of Stankevich's life and personality, and attested to the ascendancy of Stankevich over the other members of the circle. Thus Herzen is one of the first supporters of the view that Stankevich, far from being idle or useless, was actually one of the leaders of Russian thought in the nineteenth century.

Why was Herzen so much better informed in 1861 about the life of Stankevich and the activities of his circle than he was in 1854? The answer to this question is quite simple: Annenkov's book, *The Biography and Correspondence of Stankevich,* appeared in 1858. Herzen avers that when he read this book it made him feel very close to his distant comrades of the thirties, and he draws heavily on it for his sketch of the circle and his evaluation of Stankevich's role. Since we will soon deal directly with Annenkov's work there is perhaps no need to present Herzen's sophisticated treatment of its contents.

In the 1861 edition of *My Past and Thoughts,* Chapter 25 concludes with an eloquent statement on the significance of the thirties in Russian life, and even in the life of Europe as a whole. This passage helps to explain Herzen's reasons for presenting the period in such detail and for assuming a prophetic tone in his narrative:

What concerned these people? Whose breath was it that gave them new life? Not a thought or a care did they have for their own social position, their personal profit or security. Their lives and all their efforts were directed to the common good with no thought of individual gain. Some forgot their wealth, others their poverty—and they moved on, never hesitating, toward the solution of theoretical problems. The thirst for truth, learning, art, *humanitas,* consumed them wholly. . . . Where, in what corner of the contemporary West, will you find such a group—hermits of thought and anchorites of learning, fanatics for their convictions, men who, though their hair may be gray, are still eternally youthful in their aspirations?

Where? Show me! I boldly throw down the gauntlet, and I will exclude temporarily only one country, Italy. . . .

In contemporary Europe there is neither youth nor young men. I have heard objections to this view from the most brilliant representative of France in the last years of the Restoration and the July Monarchy, Victor Hugo. He was speaking specifically about young France of the twenties, and I am willing to agree that I generalized too broadly. But I will not yield to him another step. . . . Take *Les mémoires d'un enfant du siècle*, and the poetry of Alfred de Musset; just try to recreate that France which shines through in the notes of G. Sand, in plays and stories, in the law courts.

But what does all this prove? It proves a great many things, but primarily this: that while the Chinese Boots of German manufacture in which Russia has been compelled to walk for 150 years may have rubbed many a callus, yet it's clear that the bones of the feet have not been harmed. For whenever Russia manages to stretch her limbs, new and fresh forces appear. This is not a guarantee of the future, but it makes that future wholly possible.[7]

In Herzen's memoirs facts are often sacrificed to phrases, or artistically treated so as to fit a poetic image of reality or the political and social aspirations of the author. His characterization of the intellectuals of the thirties as "hermits of thought and anchorites of learning" who had no care for anything but "the common good" is an example of Herzen's sweeping and extravagant expression. His account of the 1830's provided the Russian intelligentsia with a full cast of heroes and devils, and with a noble cause that was destined to triumph in the end. It is not so much the history of an epoch as it is a romantic political document motivated and informed by Herzen's own faith in a future Russian democratic socialism. He tried to show that even in the darkest period of reaction, the 1830's, the subsurface cultural currents of Russian life were running strong. Perhaps they were; but it is impossible to know this from Herzen's imaginative treatment of the facts in Chapter 25 of *My Past and Thoughts*.

### The Biographers: Frolov and Annenkov

One of the famous salons in Berlin during the thirties and forties was the one presided over by Mme Frolov, a charming and sophisticated woman to whom Stankevich and Turgenev were very much attached. At their salon the Frolovs entertained many young Russian intellectuals, as well as eminent figures from the literary and artistic world of the German capital. Stankevich was close to both the Frolovs, to whom he wrote a number of fascinating letters touching on questions of art, religion, architecture, and Russian literature.

N. G. Frolov was responsible for the first attempt to compose a biography of Stankevich. That project was a labor of love undertaken with the help of Stankevich's devoted followers and intended to acquaint the Russian public with the mind and spirit of the great man. The compilers drew generously on the correspondence, selecting passages which showed Stankevich at his best: his comments on art and literature, his exposition of complicated philosophical concepts, his reflections on religion and on love. The method of this first biographer was to collect, not the most typical or the most representative passages, but the finest; and some of these are very fine indeed. They prove that Stankevich was an earnest young man with a lively and original sense of humor, at times very sensitive in his appreciation of literature, a tender and considerate friend, given to romantic fantasies, conventionally religious and yet quite adept at reducing German metaphysics to terms of simple human speech.[8]

This first biography was submitted in 1844 to the censorship office and it bears curious scars from that experience. Discussions of German philosophy, one of the staples of Stankevich's correspondence, were struck out by the censors. Many references to "humanity" and to social problems were crossed out with bold red strokes. Page after page was mutilated. It was probably the reaction of the censor that caused Frolov and the others to abandon their efforts to publish the biography. The project had to await another author and a more liberal period.

Annenkov's *Biography of Stankevich,* published in 1857 during the liberal period that followed the death of Nicholas I, was the first extended treatment of the Moscow circle and the first effort to assess publicly the significance of Stankevich himself.[9] Annenkov set down his memories of the notable literary figures of the thirties and forties who had been his friends and correspondents, and his reminiscences played a major part in determining the way in which posterity, and even some of his contemporaries, would look back on that era. We have seen, for instance, the importance for Herzen of Annenkov's *Biography.* Annenkov had never met Stankevich, but he was an intimate of Belinsky and a close companion of men who had formed Stankevich's circle in Moscow—men among whom the memory of

Stankevich was revered. The biographer drew on the notes, memories, and letters of Stankevich's friends: Neverov, Turgenev, and others contributed items of information. The result is therefore not solely the work of Annenkov, but rather a collective effort in which the hands of many of Stankevich's friends can be seen.

This work is a study in latter-day hagiography. In it the saint is made to possess all those virtues admired and possibly cultivated in the community of his disciples. The ideal image of Stankevich that those disciples preserved is one which does them credit. As seen in Annenkov's portrait—a collective creation of the Russian intelligentsia of the fifties—Stankevich, though wealthy and of noble origin, was a thorough democrat: in his father's home he had been treated as the equal and comrade of the serf boys, and his education at a provincial school had taught him the dignity and value of every human being regardless of class. He knew German philosophy and literature thoroughly, and it was the study of these subjects that drew him and his comrades toward the contemplation of the ideal; he founded a circle that was intended to provide its members with a source of mutual help in the pursuit of goodness, truth, and love; he was pure and chaste, and women, divining this in him, called him "the heavenly one." This, Annenkov says, was the young man who had a decisive influence on some of the finest minds of the century—Belinsky, Granovsky, Turgenev. "In the memory of his friends, and in the imagination of our readers," he concludes, Stankevich "shines forth as a noble and elevated young man"—and indeed it has been Annenkov's purpose to construct for posterity just such an ideal image. On the last page of the biography he exposes the mythopoeic mechanism:

There are many examples in Russian history of young men who for a brief moment shed a light about them, then are snatched away in untimely death.... Though we may expose ourselves to the reproach of complacent superstition by suggesting such a thing, it is possible to believe, when studying such figures, that the youthful forces which live in our people send forth from time to time a part of their excessive wealth in the form of these rich but fast-fading organisms.... The stream of our national life offers us, in the persons of these selected people, perfect and striking examples for the imitation of each new young generation as it begins its public life. Shining ideals are set up before each detachment of our country's future leaders, as models that the young should strive to emulate in order to realize their potentialities and fulfill society's expectations.

In presenting the correspondence of Stankevich, Annenkov adopted Frolov's method, selecting those passages that showed Stankevich in the most favorable light. Though he published somewhat fuller excerpts than did Frolov, he censored the letters heavily. Slight changes in wording were made in many places, for Stankevich often used informal or slangy phrases, and a saint must use proper and serious speech. For instance, instead of "After you took off from here," Stankevich is made to say "After your departure." Annenkov dropped a number of passages in which Stankevich speaks lightly of weighty philosophical problems. Passages of ribald or obscene abuse addressed in a friendly spirit to some of his comrades were expunged from the letters. The pure and chaste young man's paramour, a German girl named Berta who lived with him while he was a student in Berlin, disappeared without a trace from Annenkov's version of the letters. Moreover, Annenkov did not include in his selection some letters in which Stankevich appears in the role of a conspirator working secretly to liberate Varvara Bakunin from her husband. No shadow of realistic human detail mars the image of the "beautiful soul" created by Annenkov for the edification of Russian youth. Stankevich is denied sexual desire, deprived of his own casual idiom, cleared of complicity in the "liberation of Varvara," and absolved of any levity in his attitude toward philosophy. In his zeal Annenkov even forbids Stankevich a faintly scatological joke on the subject of one of the great disputed issues of Russian historiography, the authorship of the medieval "Chronicle of Nestor." Annenkov omits from one of Stankevich's letters this jocular anecdote: "Tell Stroev that I found not long ago on Unter den Linden—what do you think? The original of Nestor's Chronicle, and at the very end there was written 'Nestor, by his own hand.' But loyal as I am to my own school of thought in this matter, I took it into the W.C. with me and disposed of it. Now we have nothing to fear."[10]

# 4

# Correspondence with a Practical Man:
# The Romantic Period

We have seen how little the student of Stankevich and his circle can rely on the reminiscences of Stankevich's contemporaries; the documents we have reflect chiefly the mentality, outlook, and aspirations of the men who produced them. In interpreting their works we must remember, too, that political circumstances peculiar to nineteenth-century Russia made free and objective writing especially difficult. There could be no public dialogue concerning the character of Stankevich and the activities of his circle until after the death of Nicholas I in 1855, and even in 1857 Annenkov found it advisable to avoid spelling out the ominous name of Bakunin in print and to speak of Belinsky with brevity and circumspection. During the long interval between the death of Stankevich in 1840 and the appearance of Annenkov's book, the image of Stankevich preserved in the collective memory of his friends was never subject to question or correction—and it was this collective memory that produced not only Annenkov's *Biography,* but also Herzen's reminiscences of the period.

The voluminous correspondence of Stankevich and those close to him is a far more reliable source of evidence, but even this evidence is not pure of ulterior intention. In the first place, many of Stankevich's letters have been lost or destroyed.[1] His rich correspondence with Krasov, Kliushnikov, Efremov, Granovsky, and others exists only in part. Little of Stankevich's correspondence with Belinsky survives.

On the other hand, the letters to his parents, and to his brothers and sisters, cherished as a family treasure, have come down to us almost intact; but they hold only limited interest in comparison with the lost letters to Belinsky. Ironically enough, the one most methodical in preserving the legacy of Stankevich's letters was the sentimental Neverov, who was perhaps least able to appreciate them.[2] We must suppose, then, a certain selectivity not always in the interest of historic truth at work in the preservation of Stankevich's correspondence for posterity.

The problem of self-censorship presents another difficulty in our evaluation of Stankevich's correspondence. Though these letters were private, any correspondent in those times knew that his messages might be opened by a representative of the government or read in a group of his own friends. When Stankevich falls into cryptic expression in referring to Belinsky, Mickiewicz, or Chaadaev, it is clear that he does so for fear the letters may come under official scrutiny.[3]

It is true that none of the correspondence we consider here was written with the thought of eventual publication. The letter-writers did not think of themselves as important enough to be read by future generations, and so we are not dealing with literary or philosophical compositions in epistolary form.[4] But the correspondents did expect to be read by their contemporaries, and at times this vitiated the immediacy of their expression. Moreover, they were conscious of a long tradition of literature in the form of letters. *Werther, La Nouvelle Héloïse, Pamela,* and Karamzin's sentimental productions were models always available for conscious or unconscious imitation. Thus it would probably be a mistake to judge Stankevich's personality by the sentimental self-concern and gentle, "Wertherish" plaints to be found in his earliest letters: the literary models may well have proved irresistible.

With these cautions in mind we shall examine the extant correspondence in order to see whether a clear and consistent account of Stankevich and his circle can be based upon it. The principal problems are those of method and viewpoint. One might, as some students have done, select at random interesting and significant passages from Stankevich's letters and allow an apparently authentic portrait of the man to emerge from them. Or passages devoted to philosophy and literature might be excerpted from the correspondence with the intent of presenting his views on those subjects systematically. But neither of these methods would yield satisfactory results, for the correspondence is inconsistent in its presentation of the personality of the writer, and on no subject are his "views" fully and definitively expressed. However, if we approach him as the center of a circle and examine through his letters his relationship with the other members, we may be able to see how these young thinkers influenced one another. In order to analyze the correspondence in this way it will be necessary to examine not only the letters themselves but the characters and careers of the men to whom they were written. For there was more than one Stankevich, and we shall see that the Stankevich who confided in Neverov was quite different from the man who corresponded with Bakunin, Belinsky, or Granovsky. Indeed, several distinct portraits of Stankevich could be sketched, each one based on a particular set of letters. Though by no means a chameleon, Stankevich had in high measure the ability to adjust himself to the personality and the particular needs of each of his friends. Thus each of the correspondents was to a certain degree the author of the letters addressed to him. In our quest for Stankevich, therefore, we shall examine not only the letters he wrote but also the men who received them. Let us turn first to his comrade and confidant, Yanuarii Neverov.

Yanuarii M. Neverov graduated from Moscow University in 1833 (a year before Stankevich), and went immediately to St. Petersburg, where he began building a career in the Ministry of Public Education. He served for a time on the editorial board of the Ministry's *Journal,* held various positions of importance, was made a director of public schools in the Caucasus, and eventually became a member of the Council of the Ministry of Public Education. Neverov was a solid citizen of the Russian Empire whose career, though not brilliant, was fruitful.[5] The image of Stankevich remained with him all his life as an ideal and an inspiration, and about a fourth of Stankevich's surviving letters are those preserved by Neverov. A methodical man, he assembled all of these, together with certain other documents concerning Stankevich's death, and bound all of them into a volume which he kept with him always as a holy treasure.[6]

During his student days at Moscow University, Neverov was a frequent visitor to Stankevich's quarters. Like many of Stankevich's friends, Neverov was a young man of humble and impecunious origin who achieved education and a position in life through his own efforts and against great odds. He was dependent on either government funds or the patronage of wealthy friends for support during his years at the University. Patrons willing to help able young men were, according to Neverov's testimony, fairly numerous in Moscow in the thirties. It was the custom in many wealthy houses to grant protection to poor students, taking them in not as tutors or as servants, but simply as "companions." The wealthy Melgunov household granted such aid and protection to Neverov.[7]

Though he did complete his formal schooling, Neverov bears some of the characteristic marks of the *autodidacte*. He engaged in a serious and relentless search for knowledge. French he could read and speak—somehow. English he read, but he could not recite Byron so as to be understood by a speaker of English. In his autobiographical sketch he relates stories of his home life that reveal the low cultural level of his immediate family and convey his revulsion at the scenes of cruelty he witnessed as a boy on his grandfather's property.[8] His autobiographical sketch and the few letters of his that survive reveal a humorless young man intent on knowledge and serious work.

That he had little taste or judgment in literary matters has already been revealed in his estimate of Stankevich as a second Pushkin. In a letter to Stankevich from St. Petersburg (published here in part for the first time) he gives further evidence of uninformed taste when he attempts to evaluate Gogol's comedy *The Inspector-General*: "It is funny but really quite trivial, and there is nothing in it to rave about, though it's being praised to the skies. There is no drama, and no comedy at all.... Is it possible to construct a comedy out of such materials?"[9]

The critical reviews Neverov regularly wrote for the *Journal of the Ministry of Education* showed modesty, restraint, fairness, and a conservative outlook. His literary opinions were far more cautious than the avant-garde pronouncements of Stankevich or Belinsky.

It is a curious paradox that some of the most romantic and self-consciously poetic passages in Stankevich's correspondence occur in his letters to Neverov, who was a positive and a prosaic man. Perhaps this is because the correspondence was of long duration and began when Stankevich was still given to youthful posing. The psychological factors in Stankevich's relation with Neverov are paradoxical and complex. Neverov, slightly older, is the steady and sober counselor; Stankevich, the brilliant but fanciful young man who is inclined to wax poetic. Neverov is laconic and a listener, and Stankevich values him as a rare treasure: the friend to whom he can confide at length what is closest to his heart. In one of his earliest letters to Neverov we have what is perhaps the clearest picture of the genesis of Stankevich's circle: "Come over, please, and we will chat about the immortality of the soul and all the rest. Today is Friday and we always meet on that day.... Put your dissertation aside and let's chatter—it will clear your head."[10]

After Neverov's graduation from Moscow University and departure for St. Petersburg, a number of letters express Stankevich's desolation at the absence of his friend and contain interesting expositions of the romantic idea of friendship. In one of these letters Stankevich remarks on what strange results can follow the effort to express intimate thoughts to someone who just doesn't understand. Since Neverov was the listener who did understand—or if he did not always understand did not object—Stankevich fills page after page of letters to him with accounts of his innermost thoughts, fancies, and spiritual adventures. These pages are a spontaneous and unrestrained self-revelation written for the eyes of an indulgent older friend who, because of his own very modest endowment of intellect and imagination, is not to be feared as a critic. Thus it happens that Stankevich the youthful romantic emerges most clearly in his letters to Neverov, a practical man with a strong admixture of sentimentality.

The correspondence with Neverov began in 1831, when Stankevich was eighteen, and continued until 1839. There are 103 letters, covering two hundred large and closely printed pages in Alexei Stankevich's edition of the correspondence. In them can be traced Stankevich's growth from a brilliant young poetaster and dilettante of esthetic experience into a serious student of German philosophy. From these letters scholars have reconstructed the history of his unhappy involvement with three women: the village matron who aroused his senses but not his romantic soul, the lady who appealed to his better self but whom he could not love, and a third who, though she mastered his heart, could not share with Stankevich "the higher life of the spirit." In his attempt to define the view of love entertained among the idealists of the 1830's P. Milyukov drew heavily upon the accounts of these three affairs that Stankevich wrote to Neverov in 1833, 1834, and 1835.[11] Since Stankevich was lucidly articulate on a great variety of subjects, and since he holds nothing back in these letters, they reveal not only his personal problems but also the intellectual personality of his generation.

Art and esthetic experience stand out as the paramount intellectual interests of Stankevich and his circle from 1831 until 1834, when more purely philosophical concerns began to develop. The source of the circle's esthetic interest lay in the philosophy of Schelling and Schiller, as well as in the writings of Bouterwek and Bachman, lesser figures whose work had wide influence in Russia. German idealism was absorbed by young Russians through attendance at the lectures of Professor Nadezhdin at Moscow University and through reading the German philosophers in translation. Commentaries on philosophical works, often in French, were popular, and in one of Stankevich's earliest letters he asks Neverov to send him the issue of *The Telescope* (No. 10, 1831) containing Professor Nadezhdin's article "The Necessity, Significance, and Power of Esthetic Education."* (p. 210.) This article is a restatement, in somewhat stilted language, of ideas common to Schelling and Bouterwek on the refinement of the human spirit through the experience of art. Stankevich

* The page numbers in parentheses show where these letters may be found in N. V. Stankevich, *Perepiska Nikolaya Vladimirovicha Stankevicha, 1830–1840,* red. i izd. Alekseya Stankevicha (Moscow, 1914).

soon mastered these theories. From university lectures, from talks with intellectuals of an earlier generation, and from his own reading in German literature and philosophy Stankevich had picked up, long before he began the systematic study of Schelling, certain ideas characteristic of the Schelling school. Thus we find in his letters to Neverov statements on art as the summit of human experience: "Art is becoming for me a divinity, and I insist on friendship (or love—the latter is the genus, the former the finest and holiest of its species) and art. Such is the world in which man must live if he is not to sink to the level of the beast." (p. 221.)

Stankevich demonstrates in his lucid fashion the romantic predilection for soft focus and hazy outline. "You say," he writes Neverov, "that the blue sea and the blue distance attract you. My friend, we are drawn to anything that is blue. The sea is beautiful because we cannot encompass it; the hazy distance is appealing because in it all objects mingle together and blend into the sky and the air."

Yet Stankevich often abandons the patterned expression of these already commonplace ideas and reports directly on his own emotional states, which he is able to observe as psychological phenomena. For example:

Something stirred in my soul and I arrived at that vague, half-poetic, half-harmonious state of mind about which we have so often talked. I tried to write some verses....I sat down at the piano and picked out a few chords at random, and you can't imagine what strange, painful desires surged in me. Not for anything would I have tried to express this; feeling despises words at such a moment. And this was not a sweet sensation but a tortured and hopeless one. If one is to believe the esthetic doctrine that the feeling of the beautiful is accompanied by a striving toward the infinite (well, toward something or other), and that this striving is sweet because of the hope for union with the infinite—then I don't know how to explain my sensations. My chief feeling was despair of ever becoming joined with that toward which the soul strives....Ah, well, I really don't know. (p. 215.)

The following words to Neverov on the problem of the relationship of thought and art have great importance for Russian literary criticism because they are an early expression of the idea later propagated by Belinsky that art is "thought in sensuous form":

I would not say that the poet has or has not the right to embody an idea in his work, but I would simply examine those things that are admittedly works of poetic art, and I would ask, "Is an idea embodied or expressed in them?" When I read Goethe's ballad "Gott und die Bajadere" ["God and Dancing-Girl"] I don't find in it a single . . . maxim. . . . And yet how sharply clear the idea is! The sinful soul is cleansed by divine love! Here the idea is not simply expressed, but given sensuous form (*voploshchena*). (p. 236.)

Chizhevsky has supposed that Belinsky developed his idea of art as "thought in images" under the influence of Hegelian esthetics. But it is probably not possible to show a particular source for these ideas, and it is certain that Stankevich had not at this time studied Hegel, though he had read and reread Schlegel's *Dramaturgie,* in which somewhat similar notions are developed (p. 276). Moreover, Stankevich develops these ideas in the form of his own original thought, rather than in any of the accepted terminologies. His approach is fresh and empirical.

The letters to Neverov contain an account of Stankevich's reading in various literatures during the years 1831 to 1834, and from this correspondence it is possible to ascertain that his shift in interest from literature and music to philosophy occurred in September 1834 (pp. 289–90). In writing to Neverov, Stankevich speaks of art and esthetic feeling, friendship, music, and literature; seldom, and then only defensively, does he discuss what came to be his main interest, philosophy. This is doubtless because of his understanding of the man to whom he was writing, for Neverov was enamored of romantic literature and music but saw little "use" in philosophical speculation (p. 292).

Thus it happens that the letters to Neverov contain a compendium of the literary and musical fare Stankevich preferred, together with lively and original commentary on it. Schubert, Beethoven, and the French romantic Herold were Stankevich's favorite composers, though he enjoyed Mozart's works also. Writing from Moscow in November 1833 Stankevich tells Neverov how he was affected by Herold's *Zampa the Pirate.* Under the spell of this opera, which he saw performed three times, and also because of reading E. T. A. Hoffmann's fantastic *Seltsame Leiden eines Theater-direktors,* his head was filled for weeks with various ideas for stories, poems, and operas. He found that the chief obstacle to creativity was that he conceived of artistic works as thematic ideas, rather than projecting them in definite, concrete, and sensible form. It was this predominantly conceptual cast of mind that made it impossible for Stankevich to be a poet: we have already seen that for all his efforts to impart immediacy of feeling to his lyric poems, they too are rather the fruit of cerebration. The following romantic fantasy occurred to him as the subject for an opera:

A young man who had once possessed fine convictions, known beauty, and loved life is beaten down and disillusioned by people and circumstances. He is left to himself. But what is there inside of him? His high ideals have perished, love has disappeared forever. Living a kind of spiritual death, he is surrounded by the most brilliant social life. He meets one creature who, because of something mysterious about her, awakens in him a strange feeling. She is able to foresee her own death, and her mysterious being reawakens in the young man his own mystical dreams. When she dies, she does not take her secret to the grave but imparts it to the young man. (p. 260.)

In the same long letter which contained this fantasy Stankevich revealed to Neverov that Professor Nadezhdin had suggested that he write an opera on the theme of *Konrad Wallenrod*, Mickiewicz's romantic historical poem celebrating the Lithuanian fight against the Teutonic Order in the fourteenth century. Since the subject of resistance to tyranny was a dangerous one in 1833, Stankevich reports Nadezhdin's suggestion to his trusted friend under a pledge of secrecy, and adds that the professor had insisted that all local or particular details be omitted and only the idea of the struggle for freedom be retained. Stankevich had been studying the Polish language and reading Mickiewicz. He admired the literature and language of Poland, but found its people repulsive. The sensitive young poet was no stranger to prejudice and frequently expressed his repugnance for Poles and Jews (pp. 261–62).

The spirit of the times accounts for Stankevich's esthetic elation over a collection of folk poems and songs published by P. V. Kireevsky in 1833. Stankevich's evaluation of this collection is couched in terms of pure romanticism: "Kireevsky is publishing more than 1,000 Russian songs and verses that our beggars sing. What a precious collection! ... Those songs are marvelous. And another virtue of this collection is that the songs are given, it seems, without any editing and in all their original crudity." (p. 268.)

Stankevich's interest in evidences of a national spirit and a peasant creativity appears prominently in his letters to Neverov. It was because of this interest that the poetry of Alexei Koltsov found its way into Russian literature. Koltsov, though not himself a peasant, was close to peasant life. The son of a cattle-dealer, he was given very little formal education and from an early age worked in his father's business. Stankevich discovered this self-taught poet, undertook to have his work published, and introduced him to the Moscow circle— an event of prime importance in Koltsov's philosophical and artistic development. The first of Koltsov's poems to be published under his own name was sent by Stankevich in 1831 to the editor of the *Literary Gazette* accompanied by a note introducing the new poet: "Here are some verses by a self-tutored poet, Mr. Koltsov.... He has had no education and because he works for his father he often writes while on the road, on horseback, or at night. Acquaint the readers of the *Literary Gazette* with his talent." (p. 745.) The first collection of Koltsov's poems appeared in 1835 under the auspices of the Stankevich circle. Stankevich provided money to support the publication, and personally selected from Koltsov's notebook about twenty poems which he considered the finest.

The romantic taste is clearly revealed in Stankevich's appraisal of Balzac as "competent, educated, but without feeling, without sincerity," and by his pleasure in the "prophetic tone and fantastic atmosphere" of "Laughter of the Dead," a story by V. F. Odoevsky (p. 276). Stankevich's letters to Neverov express lively appreciation of Schiller's dramatic works (p. 221), and of Goethe's prose and poetry, particularly the poem "Gott und die Bajadere," which seemed to him to express in concrete images his own idea of the all-redeeming power of love (p. 218).

E. T. A. Hoffmann was a particular favorite, and on one occasion Stankevich said: "The fantastic in Hoffmann's *Tales* seems perfectly natural, like something you dreamed of long ago. And when he speaks of art, of music—you can't tear yourself away from him!" (p. 583.) Hoffmann's interest in esthetic theory, particularly his understanding of poetry as a vision of a higher and more essential world, endeared him to the circle during the period of their absorption in the ideas of Schelling. Moreover, Stankevich and the circle shared with Hoffmann and other romantics a belief in the significance of dream and fantasy and in the close relationship of the dream state to the artist's inspiration. Letters of Stankevich dating from this period frequently touch on the relationship between the waking state and the dream, on the borderline world where dream seems to merge with reality and the pictorial gibberish of dreams hints at strange and wonderful meanings. Once he penned a "fantasy" for Neverov that presented a contrast between the ideal world of dreams and the waking world of vulgar reality, a theme reminiscent of Gogol's "Nevsky Prospekt" (p. 270).

In what may seem to the modern reader a failure of taste, Stankevich praised the historical dramas of Nestor Kukolnik, whose specialty was patriotic bombast in supposed imitation of Schiller (p. 263). However, during the same period Stankevich also held in high regard, as a man and as an author, the historical novelist Ivan Lazhechnikov, a skillful craftsman whose work presented Russian history in bright and inspiring terms.

In the literary and esthetic attitudes, theories, and judgments we have so far examined, it would appear that Stankevich was not at odds with Neverov, though they occasionally disagreed on details. On the contrary, these judgments were attuned to the sentimentally romantic side of Neverov's character, and the letters in which they appear are epistolary classics of romantic friendship. However, a rift developed in this firm friendship, and it followed the line of cleavage in Stankevich himself between the romantic poet and the philosopher. As Stankevich matured his interest in romantic poetry tended to abate, and he was not content with the vague otherworldly verbalizations which had passed for philosophy among the romantics of an earlier generation. The point at which the friendship with Neverov faltered was precisely that point at which Stankevich insisted on finding out exactly what the philosophy of Schelling was. The beginning of the rift can be dated clearly by a letter from Stankevich (September 19, 1834) in which he reports to Neverov that he has been reading Schelling's *System des transcendentalen Idealismus*. He is somewhat hesitant, even apologetic, in his first efforts to explain the usefulness of such a pursuit. The letters to Neverov that attempt to explain and comment upon the philosophy of Schelling reveal that Stankevich's mind required a clear understanding of the philosophical system as a whole and of the logic binding together the parts of the system. His progress through the *System des transcendentalen Idealismus* was slow, methodical, and critical. He was at first dissatisfied with Schelling's solution to the problem of self-knowledge in relation to the existence of the "outside" world (p. 292ff.). He rejected Schelling's definition of progress in history as the development of social means to combat individual egotism (p. 291). But he continued to read and reread the pertinent works and to refine his understanding of them.

After mastering, as he felt, the system of Schelling, Stankevich was able to perceive that the system was organic to a larger whole, and that in order to understand Schelling fully he must investigate the source of transcendentalism, Kant. In November 1835 he undertook to explain to Neverov the relationship of Schelling and Kant. It is worthwhile to examine this letter at length:

You have been mocking me for my urge to study philosophy, but this study has been in many ways a salutary one for me. It has interested me more than any other, and indeed any other occupation seems to me one-sided unless it has a philosophical significance. I am studying history, but history is interesting to me as a philosophical task. Kliushnikov and I have now started to work on Kant. We have read Schelling, and if we have not understood his drift—his dialectic—completely, yet we have mastered the basic ideas, the essence of his system. In order to elevate one's belief, one's ardent conviction, to the level of knowledge, it is necessary to master the basis on which modern German philosophy has been created. And that foundation is the system of Kant. Having refuted the dogmatic efforts of metaphysics, Kant showed it a new path. He deduced that the pure, a priori concepts in our minds are only forms, and that they must be filled with experience or they lose their significance. Therefore these pure concepts cannot serve as a means of resolving those questions about God, freedom, and immortality that are usually proposed in metaphysics. These three problems are comprehended by the practical reason—they are the objects of faith. And thus Kant on the one hand has forever guarded religion against the attacks of free thought and on the other hand has presented to philosophy a new task: to investigate the beginning and the possibility of knowledge, as in earlier time philosophers used to investigate the beginning and the possibility of the universe. Schelling undertook the solution of that problem [of knowledge]. With strict consistency he demonstrated that the beginning of our knowledge is self-consciousness. It precedes everything else, it is without cause, it cannot be proved, but is felt; and it serves as the basis of all other knowledge. From this beginning (I = I) he was obliged to build all of human understanding according to the law of necessity, and he found that between pure ... self-knowledge and full understanding there lies all of nature, in the form of a necessary link, as the condition under which simple self-knowledge can grow into full understanding. He was investigating knowledge, but he solved, as it were incidentally, the problem of the origin of nature. . . . I don't yet know Hegel. (pp. 337, 338.)

Stankevich's progression from romantic poet to disciplined philosopher led him gradually away from Neverov. Coolness and strain appear in his patient efforts to explain and justify his interest in studying philosophy. Neverov, composing his autobiographical notes many years later, recalled this partial estrangement from his friend and tried to explain it by the influence exerted on Stankevich by Bakunin, who, as Neverov thought, caused Stankevich to abandon poetry for philosophy. Neverov was quite mistaken: it was Stankevich who guided Bakunin in his first efforts to study German philosophy.[12]

The estrangement from Neverov is evident not only in Stankevich's defense of philosophy but in his statement in November 1834 that he is no longer reading Schelling and has put him aside "for a very long time," a statement which, while no doubt true for the moment, belies his continuing and deepening interest in philosophy. The widening rift between the two friends is evident in the strained rhetoric of the following farewell from Stankevich on the occasion of Neverov's departure for Berlin: "May God preserve you on your way. There, on foreign soil, we will meet, already old friends; there we will thank God for the fine feelings he has given us in place of happiness; we will thank him for friendship and for love of country."[13]

It is noteworthy that Stankevich touches upon religion in a number of letters to Neverov. Though the religious view of life was congenial to Stankevich's spirit, we find that statements about religious belief or experience addressed to Neverov are more sentimental and less philosophical than his remarks on this subject to other persons, and are concerned with the observance of religious ritual, the emotional function of prayer, and the satisfaction to be derived from devotional exercises. In a beautiful and tender passage written on November 7, 1834, Stankevich attempts to console Neverov, who has fallen into melancholy thoughts, by describing his own occasional onsets of desolation, which end in humble prayer.[14] In a letter written on Wednesday of Passion Week 1834 he deals with the sacrament of Confession (for which he has been preparing), the thought of which fills him with agreeable sensations of peace and harmony. "O my friend!" he writes, "I now understand religion! Without it there can be no such thing as a human being!"[15] And in the letter of November 1835 we have read his justification of the Kantian system on the ground that it defends religion from the attacks of freethinkers.

Though the intellectual estrangement of the two friends was permanent and basic after Stankevich finally moved in the direction of philosophy, their friendly relations continued. Neverov, as the responsible older man, promised Stankevich's father to function as a kind of guide and guardian to Stankevich during his stay in Berlin, to care for his practical concerns and look after his health and well-being—matters the poet and philosopher might neglect. They were comrades while at the University of Berlin, and the news of Stankevich's death was a cruel blow to Neverov.

What was the significance of Stankevich in the life of this Russian official? Neverov valued most in Stankevich qualities of youthful romanticism that were not characteristic and were quickly outgrown;

he was impressed by Stankevich's poetry, which is worthless, and by his short story "A Few Moments from the Life of Count Z.," a sickly exercise in pious self-pity; but he could not follow Stankevich into those areas of thought and feeling which were his proper demesne. Yet Neverov helped preserve for posterity the memory of this intellectual leader whom he neither understood nor followed.

The image of himself that Stankevich projects in his letters to Neverov fits a romantic stereotype. Stankevich presents himself as an impractical poet given to subjective fantasies, and his epistolary prose expresses fine and lofty feeling as well as occasional prejudice. To complete the romantic picture, the young poet is wasting away with consumption, and the details of his health are a frequent subject of reports to Neverov. The letters to Neverov, read apart from Stankevich's other writing, would give us no adequate notion of the young man's humor, nor of the realistic quality of his mind. The Stankevich we see in these letters is to a large degree the creation of Neverov's own romantic taste.

# 5
# Letters about Philosophy and Love to the Bakunins: The Approach to Realism

The Moscow circle, which included the patriotic and prosaic Neverov, also nurtured Mikhail Bakunin, whose intellectual genius and vast energies were later devoted to the destruction of the existing order in Europe.[1] During the thirties, Neverov and Bakunin were linked in friendship through their common attachment to Stankevich. It was Bakunin who in 1835 supplanted Neverov for a time, when Stankevich began the serious study of philosophy. Bakunin required no justification for metaphysical speculation. He found in it satisfaction for the deepest needs of his ego. Because of this interest he became Stankevich's fast friend, despite sharp and fundamental differences of temperament and intellectual outlook.

### Bakunin, the Philosopher Friend

Unlike the *autodidacte* Neverov, Bakunin was of noble antecedents. His ancestral home was Premukhino, an estate in central Russia, where the spacious manor house stood on an eminence overlooking the broad Osuga River. Premukhino is important in the history of Russian romanticism, for there the young Bakunins, Mikhail and his sisters, entertained the leading figures in the intellectual world of the 1830's and 1840's. Stankevich, Turgenev, Belinsky, Botkin, Kliushnikov—all succumbed to the intellectual and physical charm of Premukhino, where they were regaled with philosophical discussion and the romantic attentions of the young ladies. Each man became enamored of the estate and the Bakunin family, and each fell in love with a particular Bakunin sister. "An ideal household," was Stankevich's verdict, and he spoke often of the harmony to be found there. But the harmony was not perfect, for the absorption of the younger generation in German philosophy and romantic literature was disturbing to the paterfamilias, who was an old-fashioned rationalist of the French school. Mikhail Bakunin's first steps as an *homme révolté* were taken in his father's house, where he was the chronic instigator of rebellion against parental authority in the name of the free and transcendent human spirit.[2]

In his subsequent career as an anarchist, Bakunin combined acute theoretical analysis with almost daily warfare against established social forms, and left the deep impression of his extraordinary personality on Russian life and thought. His earliest intellectual experiences were shared with Stankevich and the members of the circle. Stankevich introduced him to the systematic study of German idealism and provided lucid explanations of the "dark spots" in Kant. But before thoroughly mastering Kant Bakunin moved on to Fichte's *Guide to a Holy Life,* and for many months the study of Fichte's philosophy of religion formed the intellectual substance of life at Premukhino.[3] Bakunin, like Stankevich, went on to explore the metaphysics of Hegel. In the principle of negation—"the burrowing mole that undermines all things"—he found what was for him the basic truth of life; and his first impassioned call to "creative destruction" was couched in Hegelian terms: "Let us trust the eternal spirit, who destroys and annihilates us because he himself is the indestructible and eternal source of all life. The joy of destruction is at the same time a creative joy."[4]

We shall not examine Bakunin's career as a revolutionist in Europe, his active participation in the rebellion of 1848 in Paris, his plots against the Austrian and Russian empires for the liberation of the Slavs, his contest with Karl Marx, his disastrous leadership of the Lyons workers in 1870, or other events in his stormy and ominous career. We turn our attention here to a relatively peaceful time in Bakunin's life, the period when, supposedly, he underwent the healing influence of that "spirit of harmony," Stankevich. The relationship of Bakunin to Stankevich and Belinsky during this period is revealed with astonishing frankness in their correspondence, for the friends—once it was understood that they had indeed achieved the exalted status of "friend"—held nothing back from one another.

Because of his father's insistence on a military career for him, Bakunin had been trained as an artillery officer for the exclusive Cadet Corps.[5] However, in spite of stern parental objections he resigned his commission early in 1835, and in March of that year found himself in Moscow without well-defined interests or an occupation.[6] At the home of the Beyer family, who regularly entertained the younger generation of intellectuals, he made the acquaintance of Stankevich, was admitted to his circle, and soon became known in Moscow as one of the intellectual leaders of the day. By June 1835 he was in regular correspondence with Stankevich, for whom he became a philosophical confidant, a role heretofore filled by the reluctant Neverov. Bakunin's intelligence, his eloquence, and even his sheer physical size and handsome leonine features made him seem fashioned by nature to move and dominate.[7]

Even before joining the circle, Bakunin had acquired a Schellingian view of the world and man's fate. Unlike Stankevich, however, he had never actually attempted to master Schelling, but had derived his knowledge from the works of the poet Venevitinov, from casual and secondary reading, and from conversations on lofty themes with female contemporaries. There is, moreover, a pronounced religious coloring in Bakunin's early philosophical statements.[8] In a letter written to a young friend of the family, Natalie Beyer, in May 1835, he holds forth at great length on the striving of the individual human being for union with the source of his existence.[9] Since this letter reveals important permanent traits of his character, we will quote from it at length:

The hand of the Lord has etched these holy words on my heart ... "He will not live for himself." To sacrifice everything for a sacred purpose—such is my sole ambition! Don't imagine that I was mistaken when I told you that every other happiness is closed to me. Not at all. This is a truth which I feel, which I comprehend, of which I have become *convinced by the consciousness of my own being.* The life of man ... is an eternal striving of the part toward the Whole. ... Life is merely a curious journey for those not possessing a special self-consciousness; for them the external world is a mass of marvelous things unrelated among themselves by ideas of perfection and higher necessity, and constituting a formless conglomeration of curious facts. But for those who really have a sense of life ... it is not the separate facts and circumstances that are surprising, but the idea which they express. ... And what is this idea? Love for people, love for humanity, and the striving toward the All, toward perfection. ... [10]

Bakunin's characteristic traits are revealed in this early letter; indeed the Bakunin of this letter, in spite of his ostensible piety, foreshadows the revolutionary of the forties. We see expressed here with unusual force the presentiment that he must live not for himself but for the general good—that he must relate his own life to the life of the whole. But this demand for union in "love" is stated in purely abstract terms, and as so often happens in Bakunin's philosophical works, there is a profound temperamental aversion to the particular, the concrete, and the real. In his thought, idea triumphs over form; and in his life, the ideas of absolute freedom, of creative destruction, or of the pan-Slavic community were pursued with fanatical violence and complete self-sacrifice, in defiance of stubborn reality. That the child is father to the man is curiously borne out in this early philosophical letter couched in the learned idiom of the German romantics.

Stankevich welcomed Bakunin as a kindred spirit. He spoke to Neverov of this "pure and noble soul," and Bakunin then wrote to Neverov, seeking to become his friend (though friendship was hardly possible, given the pronounced differences of temperament between them). [11]

Stankevich was instrumental in persuading Bakunin to devote himself to philosophy. At one point Bakunin was inclined to comply with his father's wishes and accept the position of special assistant to the governor of Tver Province. [12] But at that juncture Stankevich sent him a lucid disquisition on the contrast between the mechanical forms of government activity and the free creative life of the mind. This letter boldly defends the intellectual life against the demands of vulgar practicality. It is one of the most interesting in the correspondence because it reveals the clear, realistic thinking of Stankevich in contrast to Bakunin's otherworldly abstraction:

I would like to say a word in defense of one-sided intellectual activity. There are circumstances in which this kind of activity ought to replace government work. Unfortunately the opinion ... is abroad nowadays that the state should be a kind of machine. But a machine is damaged by time and use; a machine is smashed in order to be repaired. It is all right for lumber to lie supine while people work on it, but what of the members of a state apparatus during these repairs? ... The machine is no model for a society. A society should be an organic body; it should grow ... out of the fullness of its own strength and the inner laws of its own organic forces. We are concerned with destroying harmful egoism in private individuals, but why not give thought rather to the means for softening this egoism by ... awakening in them better thoughts, and [a desire] in their hearts for a better life? ...

Many of us undertake various kinds of service. Just as the government tries to protect the people from civil injustice, so private individuals turn their concern to the material welfare of the folk, the improvement of agriculture, industry, etc. ... This kind of activity is called practical and positive. But why not be concerned that the folk themselves begin *to think* and that they *themselves* find means for [promoting] their own welfare? ... A number of holy ideas are now abroad in Europe—ideas about the education of the folk in science, art, and religion. ... But there are thousands of voices [raised] against these ideas. These are just dreams, they say; such things have never happened. But in the first place, something like this has happened, and in the second place have there ever been two historical events that were completely alike? ... Every century sees events that never before occurred, and I am convinced that one day things will happen that no one even dreams of. (pp. 573-75.)*

This letter raises questions of practical politics, of organic evolution as opposed to destructive revolution, of popular education, and of historical processes. The spirit of Stankevich as revealed in these lines might have altered Bakunin's career, had he really felt its calm power. He may have been influenced by Stankevich to the extent that he did

---

* Excerpts taken from the correspondence of Stankevich will be found in N. V. Stankevich, *Perepiska Nikolaya Vladimirovicha Stankevicha, 1830–1840,* red. i izd. Alekseya Stankevicha (Moscow, 1914), at the pages indicated in this text.

not enter the government service, but his failure to understand Stankevich was shown in many ways. For instance, Stankevich seemed to Bakunin to be completely detached from involvement in the material world. Stankevich answered that such an opinion did him too much honor: indeed he still felt the need to live in a society and to be involved with people. The most important difference between Stankevich and Bakunin at this time was that Bakunin was given to philosophical abstractions of a romantic cast, but Stankevich's intelligence was balanced, sharp, and realistic. While rejecting Neverov's demand that the study of philosophy have immediate practical application, Stankevich saw that philosophy divorced from reality was sterile. He sensed from the first Bakunin's ruinous preference for pure abstraction.[13] And when he introduced Bakunin to the study of Kant, he did so with a healthy emphasis on the need for studying history at the same time. Such study would provide the necessary factual basis for meaningful metaphysical speculation: "Divorced from history, knowledge is dead and dry. One must join the unity of idea to the variety of concrete facts—such is the ideal of knowledge; then it becomes poetry." And again: "Practical knowledge goes hand in hand with speculation and will only thus bear fruit. Facts without life and without meaning will not destroy us; nor will we lose our human feelings in the abstract absolute. . . . Let us set to work with fervor and firmness. There is not a moment to lose!" (p. 587.)

Stankevich introduced Bakunin to the works of Kant, encouraged a serious study of philosophy, and helped him through the obscurities of Kant's thought (p. 578). There is an occasional note of condescension in Stankevich's letters at times when he is able to introduce a refinement into Bakunin's thought or rescue him from a verbal trap (p. 579). He warns Bakunin of the difficulties Kant will present to one not schooled in abstract ideas; and though he admits that much of Kant is dark to him also, he attempts to explain the essentials, and repeatedly warns Bakunin to avoid mere abstractions by studying history and literature.

Literature gave Stankevich relief from the subtleties of Kant. He once sat up until four in the morning reading philosophy, then turned to Shakespeare. He sent Bakunin Hoffmann's "Fantasies," with the comment that the fantastic in Hoffmann is not strained or weird but "as natural as a dream" (p. 583).

Stankevich's letters to Bakunin in November and December 1835 reveal that the study of Kant was accompanied by severe attacks of his besetting sickness, and in a number of letters his metaphysics is mixed with fever. He complained that his headaches were becoming more insistent, and that "dry formulas, unintelligible by day and abandoned with chagrin come back to me at night in my feverish moments...." He recommended as guides to the study of Kant both Schön and Krug, whose "popularized handbooks...make many things clearer." During this period his correspondence was filled with the problems of Kantian philosophy. His condition was a kind of metaphysical malaise (p. 590), but he was still able to provide an ironical commentary on his feverish philosophical pursuit in the form of a quotation from his poet friend Kliushnikov, who was his companion in this enterprise: "With hellish mockery he observes my efforts to find happiness in the idea of the general life and he says of me, 'Poor little Nick.' "(p. 585.)

The correspondence with Bakunin at this point was a perfervid exercise in friendship. On the 23rd and 24th of November, 1835, Stankevich reported receiving a letter each day. The letters of Bakunin to Stankevich have not been preserved, but Stankevich's answers contain examples of the mixture of religion, philosophy, and sublimated sexual feeling that formed the intellectual atmosphere of the circle at this time. His words on the sacred nature of woman and on love as an essentially sacramental experience are typical:

Yes, my friend, woman is a holy being; she is the guardian angel of humanity.... Love is a chemical process in the nonorganic kingdom, becomes occasionally a sensation in plants, grows broader and more powerful in animals, and in man receives its highest significance—as does everything in nature.... Christianity in its purest form is the religion of love. ...Whoever preached love preached all we need know....For some, love is an amusement, for others it is a spiritual enjoyment, like the enjoyment of art; for me, love is a religion. (p. 592.)

In passages of poetic prose such as this, Stankevich reveals himself as the "heavenly" young man that many women knew him to be. And to Bakunin (also in his way a "heavenly" man, since he was certainly impotent),* Stankevich gives this gratuitous advice:

Be true to yourself, my friend: study philosophy and history.... As far as I can see, these are the first subjects I must master. And you ... are really very much like me. We have the same thoughts, the same doubts, the same needs. Do you know, the thought of women came into my head a day before I got your letter. I haven't had one for eighteen months, and now it seems to me that I *ought not* to have them. And I think it's easy to carry out this resolve. (p. 595.)

A sharp difference in the two men is brought into relief at the point when their interest turned from Kant to Fichte. The transition occurred at a time when Bakunin and Stankevich were together in Moscow, and it is impossible to say which of the two moved first in the new direction. Bakunin began his study of Fichte with *Die An-weisung zum seligen Leben,* a relatively late work that drew certain conclusions for the conduct of a religious life from the philosopher's basic thought.[14] Stankevich, on the other hand, directed his attention first to Fichte's basic thought itself, and on a trip to the Caucasus studied *Die Bestimmung des Menschen (The Vocation of Man)*, a work setting forth concisely the philosopher's system of ideas.

The consequence of this dichotomy of interest is that Bakunin and Stankevich seemed to be discussing two quite different philosophers when they talked of Fichte. For Bakunin the teaching of Fichte was a religious revelation, the essence of which he attempted to set forth in exalted, though misty, prose in a number of letters to his sisters and brothers.[15] He also gave his interpretation of Fichte to Belinsky, who in 1836 and 1837 briefly shared his enthusiasm for the transcen-

---

* Bakunin's biographers agree that there was something "abnormal" in his re-lationship with his sisters, whom he loved, dominated, and sought to attach ex-clusively to himself. It may be that too much is made of the emotional tone of the Bakunins' letters, which were written in the high-pitched romantic idiom, but weight is lent to the theory of abnormal familial attachment by the fact that Bakunin was impotent and had no "normal" relations with women.

dent spirit and his intolerance for the here and now. The most characteristic expression of Bakunin's "Fichtean" exaltation is the following, taken from a letter to his sisters Tatiana and Varvara: "Last
night I let myself go in fantasy—picked up a copy of Fichte's *Anweisung zum seligen Leben,* and sat up reading it until three o'clock.
Here is the basic thought: 'Das Leben ist Liebe, und die ganze Form
und Kraft des Lebens besteht in der Liebe und entsteht aus der
Liebe. Offenbare mir, was du wahrhaftig liebst, was du mit deinem
ganzen Sehnen suchest und anstrebest, wenn du den wahren Genutz
deiner selbst zu finden hoffest und du hast mir dadurch dein Leben
gedeutet. Was du liebest—das lebest du.' "*

Stankevich's references to Fichte are sparse and critical, and concern only the metaphysical core of his philosophical system—the theory of knowledge. In a letter written on the way to the Caucasus,
Stankevich replies to Bakunin's enthusiasm for Fichte:

Mtsensk, 21 Apr. 1836

Dear friend Mikhail! Where am I? You will know from the above. What
am I? I really don't know since reading the "Vocation of Man." Maybe
I'll know better when I've read the last few pages. . . . I don't know what's
to become of me. "Knowledge" [a section of the work] produced such
confusion in my head as I would hardly have thought possible; it threw
me into a strange, sickly state of doubt and indecision. . . . So subtly, so
satisfactorily he [Fichte] transforms the whole world into a modification
of thought, and thought itself is made a modification of some unknown
subject, and the thought about this subject is again the creation of someone. Out of the laws of mind he constructs a whole world of phantoms,
and of the mind itself he makes a phantom—and it's all done so neatly! . . .
On the road, in the carriage, I finished "Knowledge" and started "Faith."
It was a marvelous evening, but an oppressive sense of complete doubt
prevented my enjoying it. So alien and cold seemed to me this "nature," a
mere phantom of my own self; everything seemed illusory and strange.
(p. 605.)

---

* " 'Life is love, and the whole form and strength of life endures in love and
arises from love. When I know what you genuinely love, what you aspire to
most passionately, what gives your inmost self true satisfaction, then your life
is made plain to me. What you love, that you are.' "

Except for a brief note in a letter from Berlin that he is studying Fichte's *Wissenschaftslehre* (*Philosophy*), also a basic work, this is the only reference to Fichte in all of Stankevich's correspondence (p. 656). It is unlikely, therefore, that Stankevich had any part in the Fichtean cult of religious philosophizing that for a brief moment absorbed the intellectual and emotional energy of Bakunin, his sisters, and Belinsky.[16] The quality of Stankevich's philosophical speculation is again clearly defined by his interest, not in peripheral or occasional thoughts, but in Fichte's system of thought as a whole.

Stankevich's ascendancy over Bakunin as a philosopher is plain. Bakunin's devotion to German metaphysics was not that of a student seeking light on philosophical problems but rather that of a self-appointed guide and teacher who found in the German philosophers ready-made texts for his lengthy epistolary sermons.[17] Through the agency of Mikhail Bakunin, partial and arbitrary notions of Fichtean idealism, based on selected peripheral works, came to be widely accepted among the Russian intellectual elite of the thirties. And we shall see that at a later time Bakunin, after a similarly superficial study of Hegel, presented the fertile mind of Belinsky with a wholly arbitrary interpretation of that philosopher.[18] During the Fichtean and Hegelian periods in the life of the circle, the leading influence was no longer Stankevich but Bakunin; and as a matter of fact, Stankevich vigorously objected in his letters from Berlin to the distortions of Hegel's thought introduced by Bakunin and eagerly taken up by Belinsky and others under Bakunin's influence.[19]

Though Bakunin valued and admired Stankevich, though he was ready to acknowledge that Stankevich "was greater than any of the rest of us," a man "not to be measured by the normal rules," yet he was influenced only superficially by Stankevich's mind and personality, and even before Stankevich's death was already moving in a direction quite different from that of his "mentor and guide."

## The Two Sisters

The Bakunin family estate at Premukhino was alive with intellectual and emotional activity during the decade of the thirties. In his biography of Bakunin, E. H. Carr has made excellent use of the voluminous material in the Premukhino archives, and for his knowledge of these archives he is indebted to Kornilov's *Molodye gody Mikhaila Bakunina* (*The Early Years of Mikhail Bakunin*), where we find detailed evidence of Mikhail's intrigues against his parents, the unhappy love affair of Stankevich and Liuba Bakunin, and the elaborate plans laid by the Moscow circle to free Varvara Bakunin from a lawful though cloddish spouse.[20] The intrigues, the love affair, and the "liberation of Varvara" engaged the interest and efforts of the entire circle. These mental and emotional upsets were closely related to the romantic philosophy of the 1830's. Each episode in its own way served to express the need of the younger generation to liberate itself, in matters of the heart, from the forms of conventional practice and the demands of rational calculation.

Stankevich's love affair with Liuba Bakunin was one of three described in his correspondence. In each affair he sought a concrete object for love, "the highest and best means whereby a man is enabled to feel his unity with the world." In his relations with women Stankevich sought a spiritual experience not requiring sexual activity, though related to sex as part of a complex emotional whole. His pattern was "feminine" rather than "masculine." His first love affair failed to satisfy the needs of his spirit, though the young married woman involved was ready for physical surrender. Because he did not feel that she possessed intelligence or depth of feeling, their nocturnal meetings and passionate (but partial) embraces left him with the certainty that his companion was incapable of real love and was merely amusing herself with him (pp. 239, 240, 241, 243). He withdrew from the affair, having preserved his own serenity and a pure, unspoiled vision of beauty:

She's not very well educated, though not stupid; she is simple, but without deep feeling. I loved her, and my fancy left with me a marvelous ideal. Now I love a vision, and I love her because she reminds me of the vision. . . . I love her more when we're not seeing one another. . . . (p. 241.)

In each of the three affairs Stankevich, however high his motives and chaste his behavior, trifled with the affections of the woman involved. The country woman of the first affair, who was married and so had no recourse against him, developed symptoms of nervous irritation (p. 243). The lady involved in the second affair, Natalie Beyer, was high-strung, full of romantic feeling, and quite "capable of love."[21] Stankevich, with no serious intentions, sought the pleasure of "brotherly converse" with Natalie, but soon found himself the center of an emotional storm. This won him the bad opinion of the young lady's family and friends, who suspected him of incautious and perhaps improper behavior.[22] Once more he had not behaved according to the conventional pattern, and he was obliged to beg the forgiveness of the young lady's mother for the hopes he had unintentionally aroused, then disappointed (p. 439).

The third affair followed a similar pattern, though Stankevich's emotional involvement this time was deeper, and his difficulties more prolonged. He believed at first that Liuba, the older sister of Bakunin, was his womanly ideal. He allowed himself to become the object of her simple devotion, and without approaching her father or receiving the blessing of his own family he declared his love and initiated a correspondence with her on lofty themes. Such free and unconventional behavior aroused the alarm and suspicion of the Bakunin family at Premukhino. When their apprehensions were communicated to Stankevich he took the conventional steps appropriate to the circumstances, and after an unexplained and probably unnecessary delay, he secured his father's permission to marry Liuba Bakunin.[23]

At the very time when he was proceeding, under heavy social pressure, to contract such a solemn obligation, Stankevich discovered that he had been mistaken, and that what he felt in the presence of Liuba Bakunin was not, after all, love. Even as he was making this shattering discovery, he still took pains that his behavior should seem to be that of a respectful suitor aware of the amenities and serious in his intentions. He was so careful to seem a proper gentleman that he actually became formally betrothed, and insisted to the end on social punctilio.[24]

But further than that he could not go. Marriage for anything but love—for convenience, for profit, as a duty, or for some other good reason—would have been a betrayal of what he believed in.[25] Liuba

Bakunin, who lacked both intellectual and emotional scope, could never be his spiritual companion; therefore, the marriage must not take place.

Stankevich's first tactic for nullifying his engagement seems to have been to discourage Liuba by the coldness of his epistolary demeanor, in the hope, perhaps not fully conscious, that she herself would withdraw. On January 16, 1837, he wrote to her,[26] ostensibly to quiet her fears as to his ultimate decision, pointing out that the matter was then in the hands of his father and uncle, "who will surely want to insure my happiness" (p. 503). On January 17 he tried to reassure her regarding her faults (she was not an angel, she had told him), and included a fine lecture on love:

They say that your parents are in a disagreeable state of mind. I beg you, don't be upset by this, and don't think that I am upset. Be calm, take care of yourself, for the sake of my happiness and our love. Everything else must serve love, everything must submit to it. Love is highest in rank among all the feelings; it is the crown of creation. For love one forgets all other ties, all relationships, all obligations. Love shatters all bonds. (p. 504.)

Stankevich would be willing enough to abandon this romantic doctrine later on, but for the present it served him as weapon and defense. The passage was meant to imply that Liuba was too much attached to father and family, and that consequently her love for Stankevich was imperfect. On January 20 he taxed her severely with concealing from him the truth about her state of mind (pp. 506–7). On January 24 he reassured her again, saying that his father would surely reach a "favorable decision about the marriage." Ten days later he wrote a detailed and moving account of an evening at the theater with Belinsky, where the two had seen Mochalov in the title role of *Hamlet* (pp. 509–11). Stankevich described Hamlet as one of his favorite characters, then went on to speak of Belinsky in the language of love—a language he never used in speaking to or about Liuba: "I sat with Belinsky, and that doubled my enjoyment. We understand one another so well, and I sympathize with him in so many things, that sometimes it really seems we are a single soul." (pp. 509–11.) Follow-

ing this, Stankevich gave Liuba a sensitive and original interpretation of the character of Ophelia, noting that the interpretation might
well have been suggested to him by the character of a real person of
his acquaintance. The real person, of course, was Liuba, who could
not have failed to understand the reference to herself:

Ophelia is pure, tender, and innocent, and one of those souls who never
lose their innocence. She has a childlike attachment to her father and
brother, and this attachment has been her whole life and all her happiness.
When she becomes dimly conscious of a new feeling, she tries to harmo-
nize that feeling with her earlier life; she is even ready to lock this new
feeling up inside herself so as not to overstep the bounds of obedience to
her father. The counsel of her brother (those stupid folk always interfere)
strengthens her decision. . . . She decides to be more circumspect; at her
father's command she returns Hamlet his gifts and his letters, and in great
grief hears his mad words: "I never loved you." These words were capable
of wounding her deeply, but could not drive her mad. Only the sudden
and violent death of her father could do that. . . .

The description of Ophelia's brother, one of "those stupid folk who
always interfere," is almost certainly meant to refer to Mikhail Bakunin, whose tenacious and insistent interference in the affairs of his
sisters was already notorious.[27] Liuba could hardly have missed the
unsubtle hints contained in the comparison of herself ("too closely
bound to father and family") to Ophelia—the girl to whom Hamlet
said, "I never loved you." Stankevich even went on to point out his
close affinity with Hamlet, and then closed the letter with a few cryptic lines of cold disapproval: "I am unable to defend you against the
Beyers, especially since certain of your letters to Mikhail and to me
make it impossible to justify your behavior."

Cruel though this letter was in its effect on Liuba Bakunin, it may
not have been intended to wound her. Stankevich, under emotional
strain as the result of his false position, reduced to his bed with a
severe attack of the old illness, and often in delirium, may unconsciously have revealed the true state of his feelings in these ominous
comments on the fate of Ophelia (pp. 516, 528–30). The commentary
on Hamlet was followed two weeks later by Stankevich's reflections
on his own melancholic state of mind: "It seems to me that I live in

an inn of some sort, and that I am on some long journey, whither bound I know not." (p. 513.) The same letter expresses mild dissatisfaction with Liuba's simple efforts at self-improvement, and analyzes for her the source of all imperfections—lack of love: "You say you are working to improve yourself. Do you know, work on your embroidery frames would be more useful.... A person should not try to correct individual faults, but should notice the general source from which they all arise. And there is one source of all our weaknesses— lack of love." (p. 513.)

A week later, on February 22, 1837, Stankevich answered Liuba's questions about the death of Pushkin, who had recently been mortally wounded in a duel over the affections of his wife. In Stankevich's account of Pushkin's last moments, all details except those concerned with Pushkin's unloving wife were eliminated, and a thinly disguised lecture on the dangers of marriage without love was appended. The lecture concluded with the following moral: "An unpleasant, a fearful thought is that of belated disillusionment." (p. 514.) The words are ostensibly about Goncharova, the wife of Pushkin, and the disillusionment referred to is that of a woman deceived in her imagined love for a man, but once again, as in the letter about Hamlet and Ophelia, Stankevich describes the situation in terms that apply to his own expected disenchantment. The words do double duty, in that they serve, too, to warn Liuba against the fate that would await her should she marry without love.

It was the practice of the Bakunin sisters to read, sometimes in a family group, the letters of Stankevich to Liuba. Understandably, these letters raised doubts in their minds about the nature of Stankevich's feelings for Liuba. Both Tatiana and Alexandra told Mikhail Bakunin of their alarm at the mixture of coldness and affectation they detected in these letters, and both sisters expressed concern for Liuba's welfare.[28] Tatiana wrote to the Beyer family of Liuba's doubts, and the Beyers showed her letter to Stankevich. He answered Liuba directly: "I believe in you with all my soul.... But what about you? ... You doubt my love, and all the others are certain that I don't love you. Will it never be possible to experience the blessed and calm faith in one another that stands in no need of proofs, and that nothing can disturb?" (p. 515.)

A few days later, on March 1, 1837, Liuba received a message which underlined her identification in Stankevich's mind with the hapless Ophelia: "I have one question: if everything is soon decided for the best, will you be able to bear a lonely life with me far from your parents, who now mean everything to you? Will loneliness force you to look upon me differently and to see the bitter reality instead of a joyful vision?" (p. 517.) And there was a postscript, written at midnight of the same day, after he had received a first-hand report of the alarm in the Bakunin family: "I've just returned from Botkin's, where I saw Mikhail. He told me the sad news. When will you at long last believe in my love?" And two days later:

You remain for me just as sacred as you ever were. . . . It is essential to behold the world and love, perceived only dimly in the universe as a whole, in a single living image. . . . Why aren't we together? We could feast our eyes on the marvelous colors of the spring sky and sense the living pulse of eternal love in nature. (p. 519.)

For ten days there were no letters from Stankevich to Liuba. The next one contained the melancholy news that his doctors had ordered him to Karlsbad because of his worsening disease. The letter announcing this carried a long postscript in French in the hand of Liuba's brother Mikhail, whose high-flown philosophical commentary turned again the knife of misery: "Le développement morale et intellectuelle doit être le but de notre existence . . . et le but ainsi que la source de ce développement ne doit être que l'amour."[29]

During the ten days that passed without letters to Liuba, Stankevich, in consultation with Bakunin and Belinsky, had at last reached a decision: he would not drive his "Ophelia" quite mad by telling her that marriage was impossible, but would simply leave her, using the excellent and convenient pretext of his health to secure a long separation, and easing his conscience with the vague hope that time or fate would somehow deal kindly with her tender heart (pp. 625–36). This decision coincided with the elder Stankevich's approval of the marriage and the formal acceptance of the proposal by Liuba's parents. The social forms had been punctiliously observed; it now only remained to extricate oneself from them in the name of higher convictions.[30]

Stankevich's consumptive condition was indeed serious, but it had been aggravated by the mental strain attendant upon his betrothal to Liuba. Not long after the decision to leave Russia had been taken, his health underwent a marked improvement (pp. 524–26). In the summer of 1837 he left for Germany, and never saw Liuba again. She died of consumption one year later.[31]

The various scholars who have dealth with this episode (Milyukov, Carr, Kashin, and Kornilov) have missed what seems to be the main point—that Stankevich knew he was not in love with Liuba even while assuring her that he was, and even while taking the steps required by social convention to regularize their relationship. To state simply that Stankevich was a "Hamlet-like" character (as Carr does) explains nothing—such characters are as common as flies. The important point is that Stankevich was caught in a social situation that required of him a commitment greater than he had intended when he took the unconventional steps of declaring his love and corresponding with Liuba. Liuba, her parents, her family, and contemporary convention had set this trap for him. Resentment of his false position can be detected in his letters to her, and the contradiction between his real feelings and the role he was called upon to play proved too much for him.

Stankevich's decision to break the bonds of propriety and "obey his heart" was not necessarily evidence of weakness. Once he had reached a decision and established a certain distance between himself and his untenable situation, he was able to reflect upon his difficulties soberly and clearly. In May 1837 he wrote to Mikhail Bakunin (in German): "This horrible catastrophe was no doubt necessary to save my soul from otherworldliness [*Schönseligkeit*], from softness [*Schlaffheit*]—to destroy that inner world of fantasy, to set me down in the real world...." And on the love of woman Stankevich now observed:

Just as divinity comes to full realization of itself only in man ... and all the rest of nature is only God's path to himself [in a particular being], so the realization of love can only be a particular love for a single human being who is himself spirit (*Geist*), and with whom union becomes a concrete fact. In love both beings are spirit, and in their union nature itself is spiritualized. (p. 626.)

This philosophical justification of the particular and the concretely physical in love, a passage which shows clear traces of his reading of Hegel, demonstrates that Stankevich was at this point aware of the besetting fault of his circle in their thought and in their lives: detachment from reality. It reveals also that Stankevich was coming to terms with reality in his own way.

In Berlin he discussed his situation with Professor Werder, a pupil of Hegel, who advised against abandonment of the marriage plans (p. 647). Under the influence of Werder's appraisal of his position, he offered Bakunin this estimate of himself:

I have never loved. Love with me was always a whimsy, an idle amusement, the play of vanity, the crutch of a weak spirit. ... Reality is the path of the real and strong nature—weak souls live always in the beyond [*Jenseits*], always in a state of striving for something indefinite. But when the something becomes definite and particular, these souls try to fly from reality. (p. 650.)

Stankevich's letters from Berlin at this point suggest that under the influence of Hegel and Hegel's pupil Werder, he had found in the concept of reality an antidote to his earlier *Schönseligkeit* and a rational counterpoise to the notion of romantic love. The following passage, written a short time before Liuba's death, is evidence that Stankevich was examining himself closely and reconsidering his decision on the marriage in the light of Hegelian thought. After paraphrasing Hegel on the idea of complete self-surrender in medieval love poetry, he continues:

Everything that was at any given time a characteristic of human nature is a necessary stage [*Moment*] in the development of spirit; each stage ... is transformed and united with other stages. Love in the middle ages was, of course, onesided, blind; loyalty even in our own time often seems a sign of limitation—as a matter of fact, the pure love of Him and Her [isolated from family, society, and history], as Hegel puts it, is inconceivable, since it involves putting limits on a dynamic feeling. But this stage develops into a higher one. In our time, "He" should be *spirit,* who finds the *spirit* in "Her."... Then there is a clear basis for their love. I don't hold to the old dream about love; I don't believe in soulmates. A mature man, free and capable of loving, happens to meet a woman and falls in love with her—in exactly the same way he might have met and loved another.... The loftiest thing in her is herself—that is, her human soul, the soul in the body, in concrete form.... (p. 652.)

These considerations might, if pursued, have led Stankevich to act on Werder's advice and to recognize in his own love situation the reality, and the rights, of family, society, state, religion, and history. But as far as we can judge, he was still clinging to his decision not to marry at the time of Liuba's death, and in the letter just quoted he goes on to protest that "complete freedom of choice" is essential for the health of love, and insists, "I am not in love, and I don't think it false to demand love." (p. 653.)

There is no point in speculating on what might have happened had both Stankevich and Liuba lived. Perhaps the Russian family, supported by Hegelian realism, would have had its due. In a letter to Turgenev, written in 1840, Stankevich states that he was, at the time of Liuba's death, "ready" to marry her.[32] Though this may have been the case, it is also true that Stankevich took a leading and active part in the campaign to liberate Bakunin's younger sister Varvara from a legal marriage that was an embarrassment to her soaring spirit.

Varvara was the Bakunin sister who first divined the true state of Stankevich's feelings for Liuba. Her letters carry the first suggestion that Stankevich was mistaken in identifying his feelings as love. When he announced the necessity of a long absence abroad for the sake of his health, it was Varvara who pointed out that true love would never have consented to so long a separation, especially since Liuba herself was ailing, and could also profit from a stay at Karlsbad:

What is he afraid of? What cause forces him to leave her for a whole year? I am impelled to speak out at last quite clearly, casting aside all false shame, for the sake of my dear Liuba. Even if he is forbidden marriage in the earthly sense, is this an excuse for separation? Liuba will be his friend, his sister—let them go together to Karlsbad. Liuba too is weakly and could benefit from the waters. . . . [33]

It is psychologically significant that Varvara, who understood Stankevich so well, had confessed to a special and perhaps impermissibly strong emotional attachment to him.[34] That Stankevich had long since responded to her feeling is evident from a close perusal of his correspondence with Liuba. In passages that refer to Varvara he expresses a warmth of interest and understanding reserved for members of the inner circle, in striking contrast with his tone to Liuba:

At times I have listened silently to her verses, her music, sometimes (I must confess) to her letters, and thanked the fate that made it possible for her to know herself better and to seek everything within herself. This state has seemed to me the ideal existence for a man, and it is an even greater ideal for the woman who is capable of it. (p. 523.)

And when the time came to free Varvara from an unloved spouse, Stankevich became one of the prime movers in the undertaking, not only supplying advice and urgent instructions touching her trip abroad and possible divorce, but even offering to defray the expense of her journey (pp. 663–67).

Varvara Alexandrovna resembled Stankevich in her intellectual interests and her native gifts. She had musical and literary talents, and a mind capable of struggling with religious and philosophical problems, and she possessed the gift of poetic expression. Her letters on religion and love are on a level with those of Bakunin and Stankevich, and constitute important evidence of the spirit of the age.[35] A young girl of deep religious needs, she suffered at an early age from doubt and scruple, and found no solace either in orthodoxy or in her father's eighteenth-century indifference. Having become deeply immersed in the devotional writings of St. Francis de Sales, she moved for a time toward Catholicism, but bridled at the stern and unnatural demands that this religion seemed to make upon the flesh. Nevertheless, her religious spirit impelled her to certain mortifications, and as a young woman she fasted and did penance to excess. She describes her state of mind, a familiar one in the literature of religious experience, in a number of moving passages:

From the time I was thirteen . . . I was the victim of doubt and despair. . . . Even now it is frightening to think about it. I remember once when I was fifteen I was rolling on the floor, my teeth clenched tight, covered with cold sweat, trying to stifle a frightful inward cry. . . . It seemed to me that there was a loud cry inside of me: "There is no God! You're going crazy! Who are you praying to? No one hears! You're going crazy!"

At another time she felt the demands of God as despotic and inimical to life itself: "Love was criminal in my eyes, for I thought God wanted me to sacrifice all my feelings to him . . . so that he alone could rule in my heart."[36]

Varvara's religious needs were satisfied neither by the Orthodox religion nor by Catholicism. The faith she embraced for a time was the religion of universal love revealed by her brother Mikhail, and based, as we have seen, on his perusal of the writings of Fichte. The exalted and mystical urge to find communion with the Absolute through love, while it lifted her spirit and settled her doubts, made impossible the marriage she had earlier contracted with M. M. Dyakov, a Tver landowner, who, though an honest man, was incapable of distinguished intellectual or emotional experience.

Varvara's betrothal to Dyakov had taken place late in 1834, in the midst of an embittered campaign by the younger generation against their father's plan to dispose of Liuba's affections as befitted a despotic patriarch. Varvara did not love Dyakov; in marrying him she had sacrificed herself to the cause of family harmony and to Liuba's happiness.[37] Her father, content that at least one of his marriageable daughters was "making a good match," relented in his demand that Liuba select an approved suitor from a list which he had given her. Peace was restored—for a time—to the nest at Premukhino, but Varvara's sudden and strange sacrifice poisoned her own life and that of her quite blameless husband.[38]

It has usually been assumed that the campaign for the "liberation of Varvara" was largely the work of Bakunin, who treated it as an episode in the struggle for human freedom, and therefore saw to it that not only family and friends, but members of the circle and even outsiders became involved.[39] Varvara's deliverance from an "animal" existence without love, without Spirit, without God, is the topic of impassioned discussion in the letters of Stankevich, Belinsky, and Bakunin, even though her marriage had been sanctified by family, church, and state, and confirmed by the birth of a son. The struggle to save a single human personality, incidentally a woman, from heavy bondage to social forms is the essence of the "liberation of Varvara." However active and insistent Bakunin was in effecting this, it is a mistake to suppose that he was the sole instigator, or that this was peculiarly his project. The plan was supported by the circle as a whole, but the chief instigator was Varvara herself, to whom the physical caresses of a spiritual stranger had become unbearable. However, there is no doubt that the most effective agent in Varvara's temporary liberation was Nikolai Stankevich, who quietly but persistently advised, urged and aided her in the direction of Europe and a rendezvous with himself. Although Stankevich was still betrothed to Liuba the letters he wrote to Varvara from Rome are love letters in the serene idiom of the German romantics, and Bakunin, writing to the Beyers shortly after Stankevich's death, maintained that Stankevich and Varvara had declared their love for one another "without any base evasions."

Varvara made efforts to convert her husband to her own non-Orthodox religious view of life, but when it became obvious that she would not succeed in this, she used the pretext of their son's poor health to travel to western Europe. Surprisingly enough, Dyakov allowed her to take her son with her and leave Russia, unaccompanied except for a servant.

In Italy the long-awaited reunion with Stankevich at last took place, but only on the very eve of Stankevich's death. His last letters to her are models of sympathy and "brotherly" affection. These letters, the only love missives in the whole correspondence of Stankevich, are written in German, which was for him the language of thought and feeling (pp. 732–44). Varvara accompanied Stankevich on his final journey and was with him when he died. Each had found at long last an intellectual equal and spiritual companion, but the bliss of companionship was brief.

Stankevich's death was a cruel blow to Varvara, but she did not surrender to grief. Instead, she reflected on this death, meditated on its meaning in the system of nature, attempted to reconcile herself to it. When she wrote down her thoughts a few days after Stankevich's death, they took the form of a philosophical meditation on life and death, and they may well reflect her last talks with Stankevich:

To die! Death—Existence, Nonexistence!... Last night I thought about this for a long time and I couldn't sleep—but I will be calm. Death—nonexistence—if it could exist—would it be possible for a human being to bear that thought calmly....

But in my idea of nonexistence there is a contradiction, against which my reason rebels— ...

Whatever is—could no more begin than end. Being is infinity. I cannot think otherwise.

Life, Existence, is spirit, is God. All living nature is the life of this God. It is the gradual return of the spirit to himself—his self-consciousness.

In man spirit has reached a consciousness of itself—but then death, the disappearance of an individuality, the immersion once more in the general, in God.... This concept is to me the same as nonexistence....[40]

Varvara's reflections on the loss of individual existence in the return through death into the general existence of nature, occasioned as they were by the death of Stankevich, are philosophical expressions of the grief that was common to all Stankevich's friends. We shall see that both Bakunin and Belinsky at this same moment were impelled to question anew the nature of existence. At the death of Stankevich, the circle moved from the pantheism of the German idealists toward a reevaluation of the importance and the special rights of individual, separate existences. Varvara's thoughts express the perplexity of the group at this moment, and their groping for some kind of secure faith. For Belinsky this new development took the form of a revolt against Hegel's concept of the "Absolute," as he understood it. Bakunin, desolate at the loss of Stankevich, was led, as we have seen, to speculate on the need for personal immortality and to seek metaphysical grounds for believing in it.

And yet the Stankevich we glimpse in his letters to the Bakunin sisters hardly fits the role of spiritual or intellectual leader. Moreover, these letters seriously becloud any picture of him as a "beautiful soul." He was an ailing and unhappy man, perplexed by contradictory emotions and conflicting pressures and vainly seeking in philosophy a guide for life. His romantic search for freedom from social obligation and for love as he understood it led him to disregard the claims of other individuals. He was cruel, and it would seem deliberately so, in his treatment of a hapless girl whose brief existence only figured as a stage in his argument with himself. He was in no condition to function as that harmonious and naturally good human being whom his friends revered in memory. At this time he was not a reliable guide for them, nor was he the principal influence upon them.

The tragic history of Stankevich's relations with Liuba and Varvara provides a concrete image of the intellectual and emotional life of the Stankevich circle. These love affairs were foredoomed because Stankevich's idealistic view of life sought to elevate human beings above the material concerns that hold and fatally enmesh them. The conclusion that he was foolish and impractical, that he failed to take account of reality, is true, but not significant in our evaluation of him as a force in the development of Russian life. The social structure that Stankevich and his circle defied in the name of spirit no longer exists, and the circle's intransigent defiance was one episode in the gradual but complete transformation of that structure. But Stankevich himself died without realizing any of his promise, and Varvara returned to Russia and honored her bargain with the landowner of Tver, her husband.

Stankevich's romantic difficulties marked a crisis in the intellectual life of the circle. His "catastrophe" with Liuba Bakunin provided an object lesson in the dangers of subjective egoistic fantasies, even in the love relationship. The realization that other human beings exist, and that a complicated nexus of demand and expectation binds them together in a social group, seems to have come upon Stankevich as a mild surprise. But the subsequent reading of Hegel disposed him— as it did other members of the group—to take account of, if not necessarily to accept, the manifestations of external reality.

# 6

## Letters to an Impoverished Critic: Reconciliation with Reality

Vissarion Belinsky, like Neverov and Bakunin, was an active figure in contrast to the quiescent and contemplative Stankevich, and like them revered his memory. No icons graced the walls of Belinsky's study, but a single portrait hung there—that of Stankevich.[1] Belinsky's influence on Russian literature and literary criticism was profound and lasting. This may not have been entirely a "good" thing, but it is a fact, and Belinsky's intellectual personality must be studied if we are to understand Russian literature and the growth of the Russian intelligentsia. That personality took form in Moscow in the early thirties in the company of Stankevich and Bakunin. The intimate relationship between Belinsky and Stankevich—angry plebeian critic and aristocratic philosopher—is a psychological and social paradox that deserves close investigation. It will become evident in the course of this investigation that although his friendship with Stankevich was one of the most important experiences in Belinsky's early life, the actual influence of Stankevich on his basic thought and activity was minimal. Though Belinsky admitted the superiority of Stankevich's intellect to his own, he regarded Stankevich not as an intellectual leader but as an ideal human being whose very existence was evidence of a rational and moral universe. Indeed, when that ideal human being perished, Belinsky angrily queried the "Universal Mind," and voiced his doubt that such a force was either rational or moral.

## The Fast Friends

The meeting of Belinsky and Stankevich in Moscow, in 1833, was an episode in the emergence of the *raznochintsy,* the "men of lower rank." Belinsky's father, the son of a provincial priest, was a naval physician who settled in Chembar, in the province of Penza, as a country doctor. He was an embittered and impecunious man unable to secure the social or economic position of his family. His riotous behavior was the topic of a number of family letters to Belinsky in Moscow. The poverty of the Belinsky household was such that the son, who journeyed to the city in search of education and advancement, could not depend on his family for help. Discord and privation characterized Belinsky's childhood, and he was an early rebel against parental authority. He sometimes expressed his hatred of his father by reciting the perfervid tirades of Schiller's rebellious heroes.[2]

Belinsky was poor, plebeian, and angry in spirit. His anger shows plainly in some of his early letters to his family from Moscow. Upon his acceptance as a student at the university in the fall of 1829, he wrote the following letter to his mother and father:

I imagine that in your *famous* Chembar, people are amazed that I have been accepted at the Imperial Moscow University as a *student*. Anyway, I value the opinions of Chembarians very little. Though I was not appreciated in *Chembar,* I am appreciated in *Moscow*. I believe everyone knows that between Moscow and Chembar there is a slight difference....[3]

In 1829 Belinsky was accepted as a state-supported student and installed in the university dormitory, where he shared a room with a dozen or more impecunious youths like himself. He endured for three years the crowding, poor food, and Spartan discipline which were the lot of the uniformed, state-supported student. Bitter passages in Belinsky's letters to family and friends commemorate those years.[4]

During his first year at the university Belinsky attended classes irregularly and received marks that were less than satisfactory. For this reason he was not allowed to proceed to the second-year courses. Also, during this first year he developed tuberculosis, from which he was to suffer all his life, and for the remaining two years of his university career he was hospitalized for long periods.[5] As a result he fell far behind in his studies, and finally, in the fall of 1832, he was expelled on the ground of "poor health and lack of ability."[6] Deprived of official board and quarters, the ailing Belinsky left the university destitute and with little hope for the future.

Fortunately, during his years as a student he had displayed some literary talent, or at least an interest in writing as a career. He had even hoped to publish a play, become self-supporting thereby, and thus escape the hard lot of the state-supported student. He wrote *Dmitry Kalinin,* a play on the theme of human freedom, during the summer of 1830 and presented it to the censorship board in January 1831.[7] It may seem that Belinsky acted naïvely in presenting this play, which contained many passages mutinous to the point of treason and sacrilege, to a board of censors composed of professors from the Imperial University.* But his correspondence indicates that he not only believed the play might be published, but felt there was nothing in it that offended morality. He rested his hopes for advancement on this first literary effort.[8] Offering it to the board of censors may indeed have been unrealistic, but it was an unavoidable step toward publication and the fame Belinsky hoped for. The play was rejected by the censors as containing numerous lines "contrary to religion, morality, and the Russian laws." This official criticism is a mild enough description of a number of speeches in which Belinsky's hero angrily defies all tyrants and oppressors, specifically including God and touching in broad terms on czars and serf-owners. The passages in question, based on many literary models, constitute a stylized treatment of the demonic rebel hero so often found in romantic fiction. It is true that the "demon's" utterances are rebutted by other

* The notion of Belinsky's "naïveté" is well established in the literature concerning this incident. The present writer feels that this reveals some lack of understanding of the literary atmosphere of the day. Satan's own mutinous attack on God in Milton's *Paradise Lost* was translated and published by Belinsky's friend Petrov in 1830. See Nechaeva, *V. G. Belinsky; uchenie,* p. 137.

characters, but much too weakly. The play has in it the authentic voice of Belinsky's own disaffected spirit, and many reflections on the state of serfdom in which the majority of Russians lived.

Belinsky's first appearance in print was in a minor and short-lived magazine called *Listok* (*Little Leaf*), to which he contributed a poem written in the manner and meter of a folk song, and a brief critical article concerned with Pushkin's play, *Boris Godunov*.[9] Both of these items appeared in 1831, before his expulsion from the university. After his dismissal, Belinsky attempted to earn his livelihood by translating one of Paul de Kock's novels, *Madeleine*. The selection of this work was a measure of his desperation, for de Kock's book was vulgar and sensational, and furthermore, Belinsky's French was not at that time adequate to the task of translation. Early in 1833, after fruitless attempts to obtain regular employment as a teacher, he made the acquaintance of Professor N. I. Nadezhdin, the editor of *The Telescope* and *Rumor,* who engaged him to write for those publications. Belinsky worked first as a translator of articles and stories, and then became an assistant to the editor himself. The work was laborious and exhausting, and the compensation modest. The following description of Belinsky's quarters at this time gives a vivid impression of the young journalist's daily life as he struggled for survival and fame:

He was living on a mezzanine in a building on a back street. . . . That mezzanine was a nice place! Blacksmiths lived and worked downstairs, and you could reach Belinsky's place only by a filthy staircase. Next to his closet-like room was a laundry, from which the fumes of wet washing and stinking soapsuds constantly invaded his quarters. . . . You can imagine how it must have been to hear, just outside his door, the chatter of the laundresses, and beneath, the pounding anvil of the Russian cyclops.[10]

It was while quartered in such an inferno that Belinsky began his career as a working writer. He wrote at a furious pace, producing translations at the rate of several printed pages a week, and eventually taking responsibility for much editorial work. Friends who visited him at the time have described him in his littered quarters, feverishly concentrating on his journalistic labors, wrapped in scarves and shawls against the cold, and coughing constantly.

Relief of a sort from the rigors of this life came to Belinsky in September 1833, when he made the acquaintance of Stankevich and began to visit him regularly at his spacious quarters in the home of Professor Pavlov. How the meeting took place is not known, though Neverov recalls that Stankevich expressed an interest in knowing the young man who had been "expelled from the university for the writing of a play." It is not unlikely that Stankevich and his friends had heard of Belinsky's difficulties with the censor and of his lonely and beggarly existence as an assistant to Nadezhdin. The point of contact between Belinsky and Stankevich was most probably their mutual friend, the "peasant" poet Koltsov, who in 1831 had found his way into print under Stankevich's sponsorship. In that same year, Koltsov had made the acquaintance of Belinsky. From Stankevich's point of view, both Belinsky and Koltsov were interesting because they were talented men from the lower ranks who held promise for Russian literature. Such men stirred his democratic instincts.

With the start of his regular visits to the sessions of the Stankevich circle, Belinsky's life in Moscow took on a new and more cheerful color. This was immediately reflected in his letters home. Belinsky told his brother of his delight in the intellectual companionship to be found in the circle: "About myself I can only say that I'm getting along all right, considering my circumstances. My connection with a dear friend, Petrov, and with many other young men distinguished by intelligence, education, talent, and nobility of feeling compels me sometimes to forget my misfortunes." And though Belinsky's material circumstances did not improve, and his efforts to find a regular assignment as a teacher were chronically unsuccessful, the salubrious effect of these meetings on his spirits may be reflected in the following thought: "The future holds no terror for me. I examine my whole life thus far, and though I realize that ... I have accomplished nothing good or remarkable—yet I cannot reproach myself with baseness of any kind ... or with any action tending to harm my neighbor."[11]

Between Stankevich and Belinsky there developed during these years a warm and intimate friendship in which there were no reticences and, of course, no secrets. Stankevich's letters to Belinsky have a quality of spontaneity and eager personal interest that appears nowhere else in his correspondence. References to Belinsky in Stankevitch's letters to others betray a special warmth of feeling, an unashamed love, which is difficult to imagine in our day, when the romantic exaltation of friendship is so far out of fashion. Stankevich's earliest reference to Belinsky in his letters, an account of Easter Eve in 1834, is suffused with a poetic aura:

At 12:30 we went out and walked about with our pipes. The weather was calm and beautiful, the sky was clear and sprayed with stars. . . . Suddenly the bells began to ring out, and all Moscow reverberated. Belinsky came over and took us off to the Kremlin. We approached the Iversky gate and listened to the cannons: the church of Basil the Blessed was suddenly illumined by their lightning, and their sound echoed along the Kremlin walls.* (p. 284.)

Stankevich valued in Belinsky the readiness for emotional response to the noble and good. Belinsky was one of those people "capable of taking fire, or of shedding tears at a fine thought or a noble deed" (p. 287).

Stankevich had a modest measure of praise for the article with which Belinsky made his debut as a major critic, "Literaturnye mechtaniya" ("Literary Musings"): it was, he said, a "good article." But in it Belinsky had developed the thesis that Russia "had no literature," and in doing so had dealt summarily with established literary reputations and had trodden upon the claims of many living authors. Stankevich noted the angry reaction of Shevyrev, a contemporary poet and professor at Moscow University, whose claim to literary distinction Belinsky had dimmed with the comment that Shevyrev's poems "developed thoughts but not feelings." In cutting his wide swath through Russian literature, Belinsky had provoked a bitter polemical reaction, and Stankevich deplored this sort of thing: "To the devil with all these polemics," he wrote to Neverov on June 14, 1835 (pp. 311, 325).

* Excerpts taken from the correspondence of Stankevich will be found in N. V. Stankevich, *Perepiska Nikolaya Vladimirovicha Stankevicha, 1830–1840,* red. i izd. Alekseya Stankevicha (Moscow, 1914), at the pages indicated in this text.

RECONCILIATION WITH REALITY

Yet Belinsky's penchant for the polemical tone was never a cause for estrangement. Stankevich once described himself as living "like a hermit," but this isolation did not preclude conversations with Belinsky, who, apparently, shared his lonely cell (p. 342). Belinsky has certain rights which few others enjoy: he "demands" or "requires" of Stankevich an article on music for *The Telescope* (p. 344). Stankevich angrily rejects the notion that he is Belinsky's "censor," and affirms the contrary: that he often submits his own articles to Belinsky for expert criticism of language and thought (p. 368). Stankevich urges Krasov to read his letters to Belinsky: "[In them,] I'm naked before you." (p. 401.) Moscow in the summer is deserted and sad, Stankevich says, and "only Belinsky holds me here" (p. 441). Belinsky's quips and sententious sayings are quoted with relish (p. 504). The company of Belinsky at the theater doubles Stankevich's enjoyment (p. 509). His relation to Belinsky is such that he naturally and normally shares "all his labors, all his interests."[12] And Stankevich is desolate during Belinsky's temporary absence from the columns of *The Telescope* and *Rumor*:

Listen you—unwashed specimen—I address myself to you. When will you return to Moscow? Alas and alack! There it is, that *Telescope* where, just like a public sign proclaiming "Beer sold here," once shone forth the mystic initials V. and B. I snatched the clumsy volume, tore the thick pages and—did not read you or hear your voice—you animal! In that horrible town of Pyatigorsk, though I neither saw you nor received any letters I did see and sense your presence in your quarrelsome articles, and my heart rejoiced at the familiar voice. I tell you this very seriously, O poisonous Vissarion! (p. 619.)

Stankevich also provided a humorous characterization of Belinsky as "Cardinal Vissarion, otherwise known as Vissariono Furioso," announcing at the same time his intention of writing under this title an epic poem celebrating the famous Belinsky rages.

Stankevich's letters to Belinsky are affectionate and full of spontaneous amusement, but one can detect in them, as in his references to Belinsky in letters to other persons, a clear note of condescension. Stankevich often lectures Belinsky on the need for a somewhat less

aggressive tone in his writings, or comments on Belinsky's relative
lack of education and his ignorance of languages, or takes him to task
for the shallowness of his philosophical views. There is no evidence
that Belinsky's pride was ever hurt by Stankevich's assumption of
superiority, or that this assumption was inconsistent with free and
unconstrained affection.

Belinsky's references to Stankevich in his letters as well as in his
published works are of a somewhat different character. Belinsky
speaks of Stankevich as a being of a higher and better order. Stankevich is a "man of genius," destined for great sufferings and mighty
deeds, and Belinsky is indebted to him for his own education. When
Stankevich took Belinsky's side in a quarrel with Bakunin, Belinsky
felt this aid as a "healing balm."

His reverence for Stankevich was not affected by the "offensive
remarks" in many of Stankevich's letters. Belinsky knows of no one
"higher than Stankevich." Stankevich, "that mighty spirit," yearns
for simplicity, and has "declared war on pretense," and Belinsky is
"infinitely obliged to him for that." Letters from Stankevich provide
"first aid" for Belinsky's wounded feelings. He "beheld Stankevich
and praised God." After Stankevich's departure for Berlin, his image
remains with Belinsky as a "memory of all that is best and most
beautiful in life." "What did any of us amount to," he asks, "before we
met Stankevich, or those revived (*vozrozhdennye*) by his spirit?"[13]
Recalling Stankevich's death, he writes to Botkin: "His death struck
me in a special way, and—would you believe it—exactly in the same
way as did the deaths of Pushkin and Lermontov. I consider these
my own losses, and inside of me a discordant voice will not be still ...
but ... tells me ... that after such blows life has lost much of its meaning."[14]

Belinsky's attitude toward Stankevich was reverential; but there
is a lack of specificity in Belinsky's references to him. We cannot see
just what it was that Belinsky owed to Stankevich. The earliest attempt to resolve this question was made by Dobrolyubov in his review
of Annenkov's *Biography of Stankevich*.[15] Dobrolyubov was able to
show Belinsky's apparent dependence on Stankevich for some of the
more important ideas that appeared in his early writings.

During the period from 1834 to 1839, many important philosophical and literary ideas appeared first in Stankevich's letters to a number of people, and then turned up in Belinsky's published articles, where they were developed at length. Dobrolyubov suggests, no doubt with justice, that Belinsky's need to support himself with his pen explains the regular appearance and elaboration, over several pages, of ideas that Stankevich simply threw out in passing. The number of these instances is remarkable, and leaves no doubt as to Belinsky's intellectual dependence on Stankevich up to the time of Stankevich's departure for Germany in 1837. Dobrolyubov finds that Belinsky's remarks on the theater and his comparison of the actors Mochalov and Karatygin echo Stankevich, and that in many other questions of literary judgment and appreciation the "plebeian" pupil seems to follow his master closely: in his opinion of the poets Timofeev and Benediktov, in his enthusiastic estimate of E. T. A. Hoffmann, in his ideas about the short tales of Gogol, and in numerous other matters.

Thus, the dependence of Belinsky on Stankevich and his circle during the crucial years when he was beginning his literary career seems certain. The sustenance he received from them was vital nourishment for his mind and pen, and as a writer he could not live without it. Belinsky himself, in a letter written to Bakunin some years later, made a surprisingly frank admission concerning his search for ideas to use in the bitter labor of earning his daily bread:

You introduced me to the Fichtean view of life, and I took hold of that view with fanatical energy. But did these ideas mean the same thing to me that they meant to you? For you, Fichte was a transition from Kant, a natural and logical one. But for me? I had to write a little article—the review of Drozdov—and I needed to stock up on ideas. I wanted it to be a good article—and that's the whole story.[16]

### The Search for a Faith

It must not be supposed that Stankevich and his circle were the sole source of the philosophical and literary ideas expressed in Belinsky's first articles, or that Belinsky mechanically reproduced ideas that he had not made his own. On the contrary, those ideas were worked out by Belinsky himself as the result of wide reading and discussion, and, in their final form, bear the mark of his own mind and personality. In his first original article, "Literary Musings," the work that drew the attention of the Russian literary world to the young critic, Belinsky sets forth with characteristic verve and sweep ideas derived from Schelling's Naturphilosophie. It is unnecessary to seek a specific source for these ideas, for they saturated the intellectual atmosphere of the day, and were common coin in the discussions of the circle. Belinsky might have picked them up from Pavlov's *Foundations of Physics*, or from Galich's *History of Philosophical Systems*, both works in Russian; or he *might* have derived a notion of them from articles on philosophy in French periodicals. It is possible that Belinsky's passages on the nature of art were influenced by Bachman's *Sketch of a Theory of the Arts*, in the translation by Mikhail Chistyakov, a university acquaintance of Belinsky's. Other possible sources were the "wisdom-lovers" of an earlier day, some of whom still maintained contacts with the new generation of intellectuals. Ignorance of German, which later proved a severe handicap to Belinsky in his efforts to understand Fichte and Hegel, was no obstacle to his acquisition of a working knowledge of Schelling's Naturphilosophie.

The prophetic sweep and exalted tone of many passages in "Literary Musings," written in the summer of 1834, suggest a recent and conscious conversion to those doctrines, and argue that a specific intellectual experience preceded the writing of the article. This experience was crucial in the early literary career of Belinsky, and it is tempting to assume, as some scholars have done, that the influence of Stankevich was at this point paramount. But there is clear and convincing evidence that Stankevich had nothing directly to do with the matter—that, in fact, he gently deprecated the abruptness and abandon of Belinsky's "conversion" to Schelling's thought. It is impossible to say with certainty what precipitated that event. We know that Belinsky was closely associated with Professor Nadezhdin, whose quarters he shared as an editorial assistant, and that the long article "Literary Musings" recalls in many respects Nadezhdin's "Literary Apprehensions for the Coming Year," which in 1828 had advanced the pessimistic thesis that Russia "had no literature."[17] Though Belinsky quarrelled with him and mocked his "professorial pretensions," Nadezhdin was nonetheless a man learned in language and philosophy who could furnish Belinsky with general philosophical ideas and a metaphysical viewpoint. Moreover, Nadezhdin was deeply involved in a study and translation of the German philosophers that was being carried on at Trinity Seminary (Troitskoe Dukhovnoe Akademiia).[18] In short, Nadezhdin was an abundant source of philosophical learning, and it is reasonable to assume that he was the principal inspirer of Belinsky's quasi-religious enthusiasm for the philosophy of Schelling. That philosophy provided Belinsky with the ideas whereby he was able to transport his readers into the realm of transcendent being. Here are some typical passages from "Literary Musings":

The whole infinite, beautiful, divine world is nothing but the breath of a single, eternal idea (the idea of a single, eternal God) manifesting itself in innumerable shapes as a great spectacle of absolute unity in infinite diversity. Only the ardent mind of man is able, in its lucid moments, to comprehend how great is the body of this soul of the universe, the heart of which is formed by immense suns, its veins by Milky Ways and its blood by the pure ether. For this idea there is no repose; it lives perpetually —that is, it perpetually creates in order to destroy, and destroys in order to create. It is incarnate in the radiant sun, in the magnificent planet, in the errant comet; it lives and breathes in the turbulent ebb and flow of the ocean tides and violent desert storms, in the murmuring of leaves and the babbling brook, in the roar of the lion and the tears of the babe, in the smile of beauty, in the will of man, in the harmonious creations of genius. ... The wheel of time revolves with incredible speed; in the boundless expanses of the heavens luminaries go out like extinct volcanoes, and new ones light up; on the earth, families and generations pass away, only to be replaced by new ones; death destroys life, life destroys death; the forces of nature struggle and war with each other and are appeased by intervening forces, and harmony reigns in this eternal ferment, in this struggle of elements and substances. Thus, the idea lives: we can clearly see it with our feeble eyes. It is all-prescient, and keeps everything in equilibrium: it sends fertility in the wake of the floods and lava, the sweet, pure air after the devastating thunderstorm; it has domiciled the camel and the ostrich in the sandy wastes of Africa and Arabia, and the reindeer in the icy wastes of the North. There is its wisdom, there is its physical being; where, then, is its love? God created man and endowed him with mind and senses so that he might know this idea with his own mind and perception, so that he might be wedded to its life in a warm and living sympathy and share its life in a feeling of infinite, creative love! Therefore, God is not only wise, but loving! Be proud, be proud, man, of thy lofty destination; but forget not that the divine idea which has begotten thee is just and equitable; that it has endowed thee with mind and volition which places thee above all creation; that it lives within thee; that life is action, and action struggle; forget not that thy infinite, supreme felicity consists in the dissolution of thy self in the feeling of love. So there are these two roads, two inescapable paths: forswear thyself, suppress thy egoism, trample underfoot thy self-interested ego, breathe for the happiness of others, sacrifice all for the weal of thy neighbor, thy country, for the good of mankind; love truth and goodness not for the sake of reward, but for the sake of truth and goodness, and suffer under a heavy cross to merit thy reunion with God, thy immortality—which must consist in the destruction of thy selfhood in a rapture of infinite delight![19]

Belinsky's adoption of Schelling's metaphysics was the first in a series of violent intellectual shifts, and vividly illustrates the narrow limits of Stankevich's actual influence upon his friend. Early in October 1834, while he was at work on "Literary Musings," Belinsky apprised Stankevich of his conversion to a new "system." Belinsky's letter has not been preserved, but it is beyond reasonable doubt that the "system" to which he referred in that letter was the Schellingian metaphysic, which animates the pages of "Literary Musings." In his answering letter, Stankevich was not altogether happy about the conversion and doubted that the new philosophical system would finally answer all questions, though it did seem to "place at a distance" the ultimate puzzle of existence. Stankevich affirmed that religious faith is necessary to finite man as a link with the infinite:

I don't know whether to rejoice or not at your conversion. Probably the new system will not satisfy you any more than the old.... Between infinity and man, no matter how clever he may be, there always remains an abyss, and only faith, only religion, can cross over that abyss. It alone can fill the void which remains eternally in human knowledge.... (p. 408.)

Though Stankevich was well acquainted with the ideas of Schelling, it was not until 1834 that he actually began a systematic inquiry into that philosopher's work. If our hypothesis is correct, at the very moment when Belinsky was experiencing an emotional "conversion" at second hand to Schelling's ideas, Stankevich was patiently reading and rereading Schelling's *System des transcendentalen Idealismus.* After careful study, he reached the conclusion at which he had hinted in writing Belinsky—that religious faith is necessary to man, whatever his system of philosophy: "Only one higher stage is possible, namely, the penetration of this system by religion, as of religion by this system. The system [of Schelling] might develop into pure Christianity.... But one must still study Schelling further." (p. 317.)

Belinsky's sudden submission to Schelling's doctrines was the first of his psychological storms, and in each case his enthusiastic espousal of a new system of ideas was to some extent necessitated by the exigencies of his writing career. Schelling provided the philosophy of "Literary Musings"; Fichte, that of the article on Drozdov; and Hegel, as we shall see, was the source of the notions on "reconciliation with reality" that made their appearance in critical articles written by Belinsky for the *Moscow Observer* in 1838 and 1839. Since Belinsky was not a cynic but a deeply honest man capable of strong feeling, the ideas which he used at each stage of his writing career he had to believe in passionately. This accounts for the violence of his preachment after each new conversion, and also for the ephemeral nature of his beliefs. The self-possessed Stankevich, on the other hand, was under no pressure to write, and could easily afford to resist commitment, and to examine ideas carefully and at length.

The Schellingian system of metaphysics also provided Belinsky with a philosophy of art. The final installment of his "Something about Nothing, or a Report to the Publishers of *The Telescope*," written in March 1836, sets forth his conception of the service that the journals of the day ought to perform. Literary magazines, he says, have the "high and holy" obligation of increasing the number of readers of fine literature. More important, the magazines should help their readers to cultivate a "feeling for the beautiful," since this feeling is a necessary condition of human dignity and is the very foundation of goodness and morality.[20] It seems evident that Belinsky's con-

version to Schelling had its genesis in his need for a faith to propagate—a faith that would not only justify the ways of God to man but
also lend dignity to the daily drudgery of journalism.

## Polar Opposites

Belinsky's agreement with Stankevich on many questions, both literary and philosophical, and his abject admiration of Stankevich's
intellect and personality are apparent. Yet we are confronted with the
paradox that the two men, in their backgrounds, in their personalities,
in the nature and ultimate direction of their thought and activity, in
fact in every important respect, were polar opposites. Perhaps that is
just why Stankevich reports that they were "as one soul": each supplied the other, as in Plato's theory of love, with the missing other
half of himself.

For example, Stankevich's approach to the project of editing the
magazine *The Telescope* during Nadezhdin's absence was altogether
different from that of the temporary editor, Belinsky. Stankevich's
letters give us the earliest announcement of this project, and report
on its progress; but he admits that he himself is working on it only
indolently and without real interest (pp. 318–19). He undertook to
translate an article on Hegel for the magazine, but never finished it
and instead sent a half-humorous letter of excuse and apology to
Belinsky. He sets forth his own negative attitude toward the venture
in the following passage from a letter to Bakunin:

This magazine has fallen so in the public estimate that it's difficult to do
any good by means of it.... We intend to devote it entirely to translations, with the exception of the book review section, for which we need
an honest man with education and good intentions. Such is Belinsky....
But I don't expect much, and work without interest. (p. 572.)

Stankevich regarded journalistic work as an inferior kind of activity
and one for which he himself was not, in any case, prepared. In the
letter to Bakunin he speaks of his lack of knowledge, and his need
for further education before undertaking practical activity for the
public good. As a member of the nobility and the son of a well-to-do
landowner, Stankevich could wait, improve his mind and his qualifi-

cations, and ponder the world and his personal fate. But for Belinsky, publishing work was his daily bread, the editing of *The Telescope* his job, and usable ideas therefore a pressing necessity.

Though Stankevich was on terms of easy camaraderie with Belinsky, he did not think highly of Belinsky's intellectual powers, or of his fitness for the practical tasks of writer and editor. We have quoted above the carefully measured praise which he accords Belinsky. In another letter of this period, he speaks of Belinsky as "a kind, good, energetic soul, a lucid mind." How different is Belinsky's evaluation of Stankevich as a "mighty soul," a "man of genius"!

Another striking contrast between the two men was that of temperament, which manifested itself in style of expression. In his own epistolary polemics, Stankevich was a master of argument, but at the same time a model of gentleness and propriety; and he could devastate his opponents by force of logic, without raising his voice. Belinsky was an altogether different phenomenon: he was an angry man. His verbal violence had a wide appeal to young readers, but was offensive to the taste of literary gentlemen, and one of these remarked that Belinsky's articles "reeked of the tavern" (p. 320). Stankevich claimed to deplore Belinsky's excesses, and in one letter we find him promising that he will "speak to Belinsky" about them (p. 368). Yet certain of his own letters to Belinsky indicate that Stankevich derived a deep visceral satisfaction from those honest, spirited, and emphatic articles with their furious contempt for the false and pretentious:

I thumb through *The Telescope* searching for your article. . . . There, there it is, the fist that shatters them all! This time it nails the notorious Koni! Take that, you son of a bitch! And again, you . . . ! There's three times for you . . . !

*The Telescope* is more interesting than *The Observer,* especially since spirit and honesty occasionally shine forth in it through the humble mask of V. B. (p. 414.)

The memoirs of Aksakov are usually quoted as evidence that Stankevich was to some extent successful in moderating Belinsky's violent polemical urge, and in restraining him from taking one-sided, exaggerated positions. This theory is supported by Herzen, who says that at times Stankevich was obliged to "rope and tie" Belinsky. Yet it is difficult to believe these assertions. The stands Belinsky took as a writer and as editor of *The Telescope* were highly argumentative and, in fact, led to bitter polemics. And the extreme ardor of Belinsky's conversion to Schelling's system was not moderated by Stankevich's cautionary remarks.

Stankevich was aware that his friend lacked "balance" and that his education was not complete. In a surprisingly stern letter we find him pointing out to Belinsky the need for further study and reading. Stankevich urges upon Belinsky the necessity of learning the German language, since without it he is at a distinct disadvantage among his philosopher friends. At the same time Belinsky's lack of aristocratic polish and of cosmopolitan linguistic competence made him particularly attractive to aristocratic intellectuals like Stankevich, Bakunin, and Turgenev. Belinsky had the advantage over them of being a democratic Russian, a man of the people, a man who, like Koltsov, combined the native Russian character with strength of intellect and philosophical interests. The young intelligentsia of the thirties, influenced as they were by the romantic movement in Europe and by nationalistic doctrines deriving ultimately from Herder and Schelling, placed an exceptionally high value on men who were close to the native Russian soil and held promise for an indigenous cultural development. It is interesting to note that though his aristocratic friends knew German, French, Polish, and other languages, Belinsky was *their* authority on the Russian language. They willingly submitted their manuscripts to him for correction of mistakes in Russian, and Belinsky sometimes offered them advice gratuitously on the writing of their native language.[21]

We have noted contrasts between Stankevich and Belinsky in background, temperament, education, and intellect. Even more basic was their difference in attitude toward religion. Belinsky found nothing to interest him in the doctrines and practices of the Orthodox Church. In contrast to Stankevich, who reassured his parents concerning the liveliness of his religious faith, the young Belinsky wrote his mother that he had no interest in visiting the churches of Moscow, since he had more important things to do; and he urged her to give up her fruitless efforts to move him in the direction of religion.[22] This particular contrast in attitude and behavior symbolizes the opposition between Stankevich and Belinsky: Stankevich lived in harmony with family and faith; Belinsky rejected both.

Stankevich was a religious man in the sense that his mind required faith as a completion of philosophy. At no point does he attempt to substitute reason for religion, or German idealism for Christianity. In early manhood, his need for faith was satisfied by the doctrines and rituals of the Orthodox Church. As he matured, the demands of intellect and feeling grew more complex, and his mind could not be bound to any particular set of religious dogmas. But a kind of religious faith, conceived of as a completion and fulfillment of his philosophic quest, remained with him, and placed him in sharp contrast to Belinsky, Bakunin, and Herzen, and indeed to most of those who idolized him and preserved his memory. The essence of Stankevich's religion was a faith in the moral nature of existence, which he expressed in the phrase: *"Es herrschet eine allweise Güte über die Welt"* (An all-knowing Good rules over the world). That Stankevich's associates lacked this faith is evident from their efforts to find in philosophy a means of reconciling themselves with reality. "Stankevich," said Belinsky, "believed in personal immortality.... But that doesn't help me: I keep wanting to believe in it, and still I can't believe."[23]

Belinsky sought answers to the questions posed by existence first in Schelling, then in Fichte, then finally in Hegel. He knew these philosophers only at second hand. Nadezhdin was the probable source of his knowledge of Schelling. His authority for the doctrines of Fichte and Hegel was not Stankevich, but Bakunin. The Fichtean period of Belinsky's career was brief and unproductive. Like Bakunin, Belinsky knew only the moralistic work of Fichte, and he did not share Stankevich's interest in the epistemological core of Fichte's system. Stankevich examined the basis of Fichte's system with skeptical detachment, but Belinsky experienced a sudden philosophical "conversion" and a brief period of exaltation.

Stankevich and Belinsky approached Hegel in their own characteristic ways. Among the Russian intellectuals, the study of Hegel did not begin until the middle thirties—after they had examined Kant, Schelling, and Fichte—and the earliest sources for their investigation were articles in French journals. "A Study of Hegel's Philosophy," a translation of an article by G. Villemain in the *Revue Germanique,* appeared in *The Telescope* in 1836 under the name of Stankevich, though it is certain that Stankevich only began the translation and did not complete it (p. 406). As late as November 1835, Stankevich wrote that he "did not yet know" Hegel (p. 338). In November 1836, Neverov sent him from St. Petersburg, as we have already learned, a complete set of Hegel's works in German, and we may take this date as the beginning of Stankevich's direct study of the philosopher (p. 368). References to Hegel began to appear in Stankevich's letters, and one of the main aims of his trip to Berlin was to study Hegel at the source. Karl Werder, the Hegelian under whose direction Stankevich studied, became his close friend, and when Stankevich died Werder wrote a moving philosophical meditation called "Death."[24] In the State Historical Museum on Red Square in Moscow there is a thick archive containing Stankevich's handwritten notes on the lectures of Werder. In the last months of his life Stankevich wrote two brief notes on Hegel's philosophy. The first was an attempt to explain to himself the Hegelian esthetic. The second was a statement of his own understanding of the highest "use" of philosophy:

In the course of study, the mind is gradually freed from its sensuous casing, and it begins to see clearly. Separate mortal existences gradually move from their fixed places, and melt away in the joyful, universal dance of life. The fog lifts, nocturnal shadows take flight, and suddenly the full light of love pours out over creation and crowns the labor of transformation. Here is life, now comprehended by mind, which at first appeared to our eye in the coarse immediacy of phenomena. Good! Have no further care for those shadows which the sun has put to flight. They were not truth, not the Absolute—and all thy labor was only a journey toward the Absolute.[25]

This interesting reflection, taken together with other statements in Stankevich's correspondence, reveals the chief characteristic of his mind: the demand for wholeness and harmony in his apperception of the world, together with a kind of "faith" (this is the term he himself uses) in the reality of something—call it the Absolute, the Idea, the Spirit, or what you will—beyond the accidents of the material world. This "something" is what man approaches through "science," and attempts to affirm and express in artistic creation. This faith in the spirit, and in the essential goodness of the universe, never left Stankevich, and after his death his friends recalled with particular interest and insistence that he never "lost faith."

Though Belinsky's Hegelianism developed independently of Stankevich, and matured, for the most part, after Stankevich's departure for Germany, yet there are certain points, psychological rather than intellectual, at which the effect of Stankevich's personality on this development can be clearly seen. Perhaps this is a clue to Belinsky's frequent insistence on the beneficial effect on him of Stankevich's "spirit."

Belinsky's understanding of Hegel was reduced to the simple formula, "All that's real is rational," and the revelation contained in this phrase led to his attempted "reconciliation with reality" and the rebuilding of his life on new and less violent lines.

### *Belinsky's Reconciliation*

A curious and little understood phase in the relationship between Stankevich and Belinsky was the period of "reconciliation with reality," during which Belinsky deemed it necessary to accept and embrace the visible world, even in its ugliest manifestations, as an expression of the ultimate reason immanent in the whole. The psychological processes that led Belinsky to this state of mind began during a visit to the Bakunin estate at Premukhino in the fall of 1836. This visit was undertaken at Stankevich's advice, and with the help of money supplied by the circle.

Belinsky's letters give a vivid picture of his tortured mental and moral condition at the time of his trip to Premukhino. In them, he tells the sad tale of his infatuation with a lady of easy morals, whose intellect he had tried to develop through recommended readings in romantic poetry. This affair had adversely affected his pocketbook, his nerves, and his morale.[26] Stankevich writes to Neverov of Belinsky's condition in a letter which includes a statement of what Stankevich considered the basic difference in character between himself and Belinsky:

Belinsky is resting at the Bakunins' from his boring, lonely, and laborious life. I am sure that this sojourn will have a beneficial effect on him. Full of noble feelings, with a sound, free mind . . . he requires only one thing: to know life in its most noble sense, by his own experience and not only intellectually: to recognize moral well-being, and the possibility of harmonizing the inner and the outer world—a kind of harmony which until now has seemed to him beyond attainment, but which he now believes in. . . . The Bakunin household is an ideal one, and therefore you can imagine the effect it will have on a soul which is no stranger to the divine spark.

Continuing, Stankevich gives us the following comment on his own character: "In me there is another lack, the exact opposite of Belinsky's: I believe too much in family happiness. . . . What I need is more hardness, more cruelty." (p. 363.) Here Stankevich underlines his own peaceful relations with family and society, and Belinsky's alienation from both. Stankevich imagined, naïvely enough, that a spell of rest at a "nobleman's nest" would induce in Belinsky the kind of harmony which was organic to himself. All the friends hoped that Belinsky would reach a kind of reconciliation with the demands of reality. To some extent, this reconciliation did occur, and the Premukhino harmony had a temporary healing effect on the wounded and rebellious spirit of Belinsky, although life at the Bakunin home was not without its dissonances and conflicts.[27] Up to the time of his break with Bakunin, Belinsky's references to the Premukhino visit are rapturous and exalted. By the invitation to Premukhino, he tells Bakunin, ". . . you resurrected me. My spirit softened, its bitterness passed away."[28] But after his break with Bakunin, Belinsky's references to the visit emphasized the elements of dissonance and disharmony that were present in it.[29]

Another important event that may have been a factor in Belinsky's "reconciliation" was the suppression of *The Telescope*. This occurred in the fall of 1836 during Belinsky's visit to Premukhino in search of "harmony." It was a cruel blow not only to Belinsky but to Stankevich and all the members of the circle, since *The Telescope* had become their own editorial project. Chaadaev's "Philosophical Letter"—the cause of the suppression—advanced the idea that Russia had as yet contributed nothing to human history or culture, an idea which was a commonplace in the discussions of the day and had already appeared in *The Telescope* itself in reference to the achievements of Russian literature.[30] But now the State, the embodiment and expression of "reason," declared that the authors of such ideas were insane, and Chaadaev was placed under a doctor's care. The suppression of *The Telescope*, and the arrest and eventual exile of both Chaadaev and the magazine's editor, Nadezhdin, were shocking experiences for the editor's chief assistant, Belinsky. His quarters in Moscow were searched by the police and all his papers impounded. When the news reached him at Premukhino, his position seemed so precarious that the circle laid plans for finding him a position abroad as a traveling tutor. References to this project in Stankevich's letters are understandably cryptic and perhaps deliberately confusing. He wrote to Belinsky: "Remember, you have nothing to do with *The Telescope*; you'll be traveling as a teacher." Then a week later he instructed Bakunin, "Tell your filthy friend (*neumoika*) that Count Stroganov [superintendent of education in Moscow] won't let him out. But break it to him gently, because his hopes may be high." The plan was abandoned and Belinsky returned to Moscow, where he was closely interrogated by the police, then released (p. 622).

It may seem at first sight paradoxical to say that this disturbing episode in Belinsky's life was perhaps a factor in his "reconciliation" with Russian reality. But as a matter of fact there was, at this point, no other path for him to take. Rebellion against the reality embodied in the Czarist state had proved fruitless and very nearly suicidal. It seemed necessary to embrace that reality, and to find firm philosophical grounds for doing so.

By the end of 1836, the manner of Belinsky's life, compounded as it was of poverty, editorial drudgery, and continual psychological strain, had brought his health once more to the breaking point. Sick

and rebellious, leading a lone, beggarly, and frustrated existence, be-
trayed and disappointed in his romantic hopes, full of bile and bitterness, he now found himself suspected by the government, and with
a cloud of doubt and fear thrown over his future. To Belinsky's
friends, a few months of rest and recuperation for him seemed a
necessity. Bakunin managed to borrow three hundred rubles, and
gave it to Belinsky so that he could travel to the Caucasus watering
places. Thus Belinsky was able to spend the summer of 1837 "taking
the cure."

Belinsky's season in the Caucasus was the immediate prelude to
his Hegelian conversion and his "reconciliation with reality," yet
during his stay there, though actually on the point of breaking with
what he called the idealism and romanticism of his Fichtean period,
he propagated the doctrines of Fichte, a philosopher he knew only
superficially, with fanatical zeal. Belinsky had many heated discussions with N. M. Satin, a member of Herzen's circle who had been
arrested and exiled to the Caucasus for an offense against the majesty
of the state. The tenor of Belinsky's argument with him was that the
evil and suffering of the world are phantoms, and that "eternal spirit,"
the only reality, must be entered into through quiet, peaceful contemplation.[31]

Belinsky, in his argument with Satin, clearly protests too much.
This was his final effort to find inner harmony through contemplation
of the infinite reality of spirit, in spite of the finite ugliness of his own
and Russia's life. His next step was to reject the mystical search for
the "Beyond and Above" (*Jenseits*), and to accept as real and rational
whatever actually exists in the here and now. In this pathetically human but quite unphilosophical manner, Belinsky's Hegelian phase
and period of "reconciliation" began.

Soon after Belinsky's trip to the Caucasus, there appears in his letters
a new note of tolerance and patience—a kind of willingness to accept
the world in both its good and evil manifestations. His former "anger
and bitterness" he ascribes to a "lack of love"—for he now feels that
even love of the truth should never show itself in the form of hatred
of the bearers of evil. He writes to Bakunin: "As you have pointed

out, in the general life of the spirit all is good."³² Here we have probably the earliest indication of Belinsky's movement toward "reconciliation." In this letter, Belinsky expresses the need to free himself from rancor and bitterness—to understand all, perhaps to forgive all. The faults of the older generation, as exhibited in the person of Bakunin's father, Belinsky attempts to understand and accept; toward the baseness of Senkovsky, editor of the *Library for Reading,* he expresses tolerance: "There's no great profit in proving that he is a scoundrel and his *Library* a filthy journal...." Belinsky notes that the published products of his own pen drew unfavorable attention from the government not so much because of their content as because of their violent polemical tone, and he plans to avoid such stupidity in the future. His newfound inner peace he describes in quasi-Hegelian terms as a philosophical experience, though at times he professes to find the real cause for it in his own improved digestive system. Indeed, this letter to Bakunin is a peculiar mixture of philosophy, sensitivity, and alimentary euphoria.

One of Belinsky's longest and most important epistolary essays is one addressed to Stankevich in Berlin and written during September and October 1839.³³ This letter is the central document on the affairs of the circle and of Belinsky himself at the close of the decade. Although affection and admiration for Stankevich animate the missive, it is, in the main, Belinsky's declaration of literary and philosophical independence from the leader of the Moscow circle.

The letter from Stankevich that occasioned Belinsky's declaration has not been preserved, but the main burden of it can be guessed from Belinsky's reply. Belinsky, with a certain scorn, rejects Stankevich's negative opinion of the most recent Russian poetry as the sad result of Stankevich's sojourn in a foreign capital, Berlin. He quotes from Stankevich's letter a severely critical description of his own style of literary criticism: "And finally, Vissarion, (Stankevich had written) your articles exhibit all their usual faults and virtues: as usual you hold forth with resonant vehemence before your reading public, as though smoking and arguing with your friends; every theoretical proposition calls for lengthy citations and examples; you try to give us, in a few lines of Gogol, 'perfect examples of art'...it's all very strange." And Belinsky's answer is both passionate and earnest: "Even though it's you who say this, I can't agree, and I'll tell you why. In the first place, for all my 'vehemence,' there was always something that came out of the fullness of my nature and that imparted to my public truths they were hearing for the first time....Oh, my dear friend Nikolai, I'm so sorry that my vehemence and my pipe conceal from you that element of truth which you could once see."

In this letter, Belinsky not only declares his independence of Stankevich in matters of literary taste and criticism, but he clearly shows that he has taken a philosophical path that may not be his own, but certainly is not the one marked out for him by Stankevich. This letter contains a definitive statement on Belinsky's "reconciliation with reality" and his understanding of Hegelian realism:

I came to Moscow from the Caucasus, and Bakunin was here too—now we are living together. During the summer he studied Hegel's philosophy of religion and of law. A new world opened out before us. "Might is right and right is might." I can't describe to you with what feelings I heard these words. To me it was a liberation. I grasped the meaning of the fall of kingdoms, the righteousness of conquerors. I understood that there is no such thing as savage material force. There is no domination of the bayonet and the sword. There is no arbitrary power. Nothing happens by accident. And at last there came to an end my weary guardianship of the human race, and the significance of my fatherland appeared to me in a new light. The word *reality* has become for me equal in meaning to the word *God*.[34]

We have already seen that Belinsky received the Hegelian doctrine not from Stankevich but from Bakunin, and in a version that Stankevich scornfully rejected. And yet it may be that there was still a residue of Stankevich's personal influence and spirit, if not of his thought, in Belinsky's "new world." For in his new experience Belinsky continued, on the philosophical plane, the search for "harmony" that he had begun under the guidance of Stankevich and Bakunin. The terms Belinsky uses to describe this experience are reminiscent of the language of religious conversion and resignation to ultimate reality—though for the religious mind, the "absolute idea," the "reason," which justifies all, is usually personalized as "God." Belinsky's vocabulary during his early Hegelian period acquired a religious coloring: the word "God" is used in reference to Hegel's "Absolute," and "holy and sacred" in reference to the Russian state. For Belinsky attempted, in his zeal, to carry the quest for harmony much farther than Stankevich himself was willing to go. Belinsky's articles during this period attempt to include in the "real," which is rational and sacred, even the "official" Russia of Nicholas I, with its backwardness, cruelty, and serfdom.

During the period of his truce with reality, Belinsky's literary pantheon was radically rearranged. He rejected with characteristic vehemence the poet on whose works he had been nurtured: Schiller. It now seemed to Belinsky that Schiller, the poet who celebrated rebellion and the free human spirit, had been the cause of his futile warfare with the hard realities of family, society, and state.[35] Goethe now seemed modest and sound, because Goethe had recognized the existing state of the world as necessary and rational, and had come to terms with it. Griboedov had presented, in Chatsky, a character in *Woe from Wit,* a portrait of the intellectual at odds with the philistines of his time. Belinsky now regarded Chatsky as a "phrasemaker and an idealistic clown." The Polish poet Mickiewicz, because he supported with his pen the political liberation of his people, now appeared to Belinsky as nothing but a "producer of rhymed pamphlets." And yet within a few months, Belinsky was to reject most of these opinions, and to feel disgust at himself for having propagated them.[36] "May my putrid urge toward reconciliation with a putrid reality be damned," he wrote in October 1840. "Long live the poet Schiller, noble advocate of humanity."

Belinsky's period of reconciliation, on both the philosophical and literary planes, can, perhaps, be better understood if we bear in mind the kind of man he was and the complex set of psychological pressures that were at work on him at the time. Both ambitious and terribly honest, he saw the need to find a place for himself in the literary world of his era, and to justify himself in taking that place. After the suppression of *The Telescope,* and in view of his own difficulties with the government, he must have felt that he needed to change his viewpoint drastically in order to continue as a journalist and critic. The caricature of Hegelianism that Belinsky developed to justify his becoming, as Stankevich put it, "more pacific," was a necessity for a man incapable of opportunistic compromise.

### Belinsky after the Death of Stankevich

The period of "reconciliation" was short-lived, and one of the earliest indications that Belinsky's faith was weakening is contained in the letter written on the occasion of Stankevich's death. Curiously enough, Belinsky now questions Hegel's "reality" in terms that recall a passage in a letter Stankevich wrote to Bakunin several years earlier, at a time when Bakunin and Belinsky were very close. In that letter, Stankevich defended the idea of personal immortality against what he supposed to be the Hegelian concept of an immortality based on the merging of the individual with the "All" (p. 624). Similarly, Belinsky now rejects this swallowing up of the individual in the general, though there is no suggestion that his mind seeks rest in the thought of personal immortality.

Belinsky's recovery from the excesses of his "reconciliation" was not directly influenced by Stankevich, though Stankevich, when he heard of the misinterpretation of Hegel involved in the circle's latest philosophical position, sent this critical admonition:

> The news about the writings and the concepts of our friends is rather disturbing. As far as "reality" is concerned, let them read about that in Hegel's *Logic*, where it is said that reality, in the sense of immediacy, external existence, is merely accident; and that reality in its essence is reason, spirit. . . . But give them only my arguments, without the poison of mockery. That would only anger them, and they are good people with whom I have no desire to quarrel. (p. 486.)

This simple, economical, and clearheaded exegesis either never reached Belinsky, or if it did, failed to hold him back from new excesses. Not long after the death of Stankevich, Belinsky produced in a number of letters to Botkin his ringing indictment of the Hegelian "Absolute," which he personalized as an alien and inimical force. The mark of Stankevich's lucid intellectual style is absent from these letters, with their unbridled, dogmatic rhetoric. There is reason to believe that Herzen was now an important influence on Belinsky's thought. Bakunin had introduced Belinsky to a travestied Hegel; now Herzen led him away from that travesty. The following excerpt is from a passage that has little to do with the real teaching of Hegel, though it betrays Belinsky's warmth and compassion: "The fate of the individual, of the personality, is more important than the fate of the whole universe and the health of that Chinese emperor, the Hegelian *Allgemeinheit*."[37] And Belinsky goes on to condemn Hegel in fierce language, blaming him for his own reconciliation with Russian reality. Bowing down ironically to Hegel's "philosophic cap," Belinsky announces that even if he were to climb to the highest rung of the ladder of development, he would still ask for an accounting of all the sacrifices and all the human suffering in recorded history; and that he cannot accept the final "harmony" of the Absolute Reason at the expense of discord and suffering.

In his statement on Hegel, Belinsky took a direction radically different from that taken by Stankevich. The latter had met and solved to his own satisfaction, within the framework of Hegelianism, the very problems upon which Belinsky waxes so eloquent and so furious in his letters to Botkin during 1840. Here the basic differences between the two men come clearly to light: Stankevich possessed, to a high degree, that "harmony of soul" that Belinsky hoped to find; he was already reconciled in spirit to reality, and needed no Hegelian dogma on the subject. Belinsky was not reconciled. His rebellion was not against any real Hegel, but rather against a universe that seemed to be at odds with human ideas of goodness and morality.

That these discussions of the thirties and forties had an effect far beyond the circle itself is shown by the fact that Dostoevsky, in creating Ivan Karamazov, an unreconciled and rebellious soul, drew directly on Belinsky's eloquent statements in his letter to Botkin. The parallels between Ivan's rejection of "God's world" and Belinsky's angry letter to Botkin are too close to be accidental, and there can be no doubt that Dostoevsky consciously modeled Ivan's rebellion on

Belinsky's. Dostoevsky, however, expunged all references to Hegel's "philosophical cap," or to the *Allgemeinheit,* and directly identified the object of Ivan's—and Belinsky's—wrath as "God."

In a letter written shortly before his death in 1840, Stankevich himself had remarked on the same problem of individual good and individual happiness that eventually led to Belinsky's rejection of Hegel. Stankevich reported a discussion with the painter Markov in which Markov had said, "For me, the existence of a single hungry beggar is sufficient to destroy the whole harmony of nature." (p. 707.) And Stankevich admits that although Markov's argument is hard to answer, much depends on the character of the individual; he himself has a kind of faith in the spirit, in the ultimate goodness of things.

Belinsky, after his rejection, "not so much of Hegel as of Hegel's Absolute," continued to use in his critical articles an approach that was basically Hegelian. The esthetic he had learned in that school remained with him throughout his life, and even the terminology of his articles was clearly Hegelian. What has been called his "contribution" to literary criticism in Russia, the concept that literary art is "thinking in images," was borrowed directly from the Hegelian esthetics; and the emphasis on idea and purpose in art which is so prominent in his later writings owes a debt to the same source.

Belinsky's disillusionment with Hegelian doctrine did not restrain him from other excesses during the forties, and the memory of the sainted Stankevich had no discernible effect on his fierce intellectual rages. He turned now to French writers, and became an ardent utopian socialist. He read with enthusiastic approval accounts of the French Revolution, and the active role played in it by the guillotine. "A new world opened before me." What history required, he said, was "terrorists of word and deed like Robespierre and Saint-Just." Pierre Leroux had become for him "a new Christ."[38] A favorite writer was George Sand, "the Joan of Arc of our time—the star of salvation." And Russian "reality," in the form of Church and State, he withered with his scorn. The following passages from Belinsky's famous "Letter to Gogol" would probably have elicited from Stankevich an urbane admonition to avoid excess:

Russia presents the horrible spectacle of a land where men traffic in men, not having even that justification that the American plantation owners craftily avail themselves of, affirming that a Negro is not a man; the spectacle of a land where people do not call themselves by names but by sobriquets: Vankas, Vasskas, Steshkas, Palashkas; the spectacle of a country, finally, where there are not only no guarantees whatsoever for one's individuality, honor, property, but where there is not even order maintained by police, but only enormous corporations of various administrative thieves and robbers! The most important national problems in Russia now are: the abolition of the right to own serfs, the abrogation of corporal punishment, the introduction, as far as possible, of a strict fulfillment of at least those laws that already exist. This is felt even by the government itself (which is well aware of what the landowners do with their peasants and how many throats of the former are cut every year by the latter). This is proved by the government's timid and fruitless half-measures for the benefit of our white Negroes, and the comic substitution of a cat-o'-three tails for a knout with but a single lash. . . .

Can it be possible that you, the author of the *Inspector General* and *Dead Souls*—can it be possible that you sincerely, from your very soul, have sung a hymn to the abominable Russian clergy, placing it immeasurably above Catholic clergy? Let us suppose that you do not know that the latter at one time amounted to something, while the former has never been anything save the servant and slave of secular power; yet is it really possible that you are unaware that our clergy is now held in universal contempt by Russian society and the Russian people? About whom is it the Russian folk tell a filthy story? About the priest, the priest's wife, the priest's daughter, and the priest's hired hand. Whom do the Russian folk call a breed of crazy fools? The priests. Isn't the priest in Russia the representative to all Russians of gluttony, miserliness, servility, shamelessness? And apparently you don't know all this? Strange! According to you, the Russian peasantry is the most religious in the world—which is a lie! The basis of religiousness is piety, reverence, fear of God. But the Russian utters the name of God even as he scratches himself. . . . He says of a holy image: "If it works, pray before it; if it don't work, use it for a pot cover."[39]

The last letters of Stankevich show no evidence whatever of analogous ebullience.[40] Toward Feuerbach, whose work, along with that of the left-wing Hegelians Strauss and Ruge, was influential in the Belinsky circle, Stankevich evinced interest but critical reserve: "[Feuerbach] has a mighty nature. There is something full and whole in his character; but this fire, this power, sometimes leads him too far afield, so that he is inconsistent." (p. 670.)

To the end of Stankevich's life, religion retained its importance for him, and we find him writing to the Frolovs in June 1839: "Religion is the demand for philosophy, but philosophy itself should end where philosophy began; the former is desire, the latter fulfillment. ... But what kind of fulfillment can there be if there has been no desire, no love?" (p. 679.) In this brief kernel we have what might be called Stankevich's "wisdom." For him, philosophy is knowledge of the self and of the world, knowledge of the idea; the demand for this knowledge grows out of religion—the desire for union with God. Thus, philosophy and religion are incomplete without each other. This message, though Belinsky heard it many years before from a "higher being," his friend Stankevich, had no effect on Belinsky's thought or activity.

The literary opinions Stankevich expressed in his last letters are on a different plane entirely from those of Belinsky. The novels of George Sand, which Belinsky described as a "divine creation," seem to Stankevich admirable in intention, but strained and unnatural in execution: there was in them too much "deliberate exaggeration and downright foolishness." But Stankevich characteristically withholds final judgment: "I will have to read more of her works in order to get a full and fair impression." (p. 679.) Here again we observe in Stankevich the restraint and critical detachment of a scholar, in contrast to the enthusiasm of the working critic, Belinsky.

There is no evidence in Stankevich's correspondence that he was concerned with the solution of social problems. Though the period of study in Berlin, and especially his contact with Hegelian thought, had helped him to see the need for relating the science of philosophy to actual people and the facts of an actual world, this new realism took the form of a renewed interest in history and literature. While not indifferent to discord and suffering, Stankevich saw no easy path to removing them and specifically rejected the idea that philosophy had any such goal. He could give no answer to the painter Markov's contention that "the existence of a single hungry beggar is enough to destroy the harmony of nature," but his own acceptance of the hungry beggar was based, he said, on temperament, on faith, and on the certainty "that the world is governed by a rational principle." To such thoughts Belinsky had always been a stranger.

Stankevich, the man Belinsky revered, had little influence on his thought or his career. It is true that Stankevich provided for him and many others a congenial milieu and usable ideas. But the tortured progression from one faith to another, the series of conversions—to Schelling, to Fichte, to Hegelian reconciliation, then to utopian socialism—had nothing to do with Stankevich. Belinsky would have been a very different writer and critic had his nature been open to influence from his admired contemporary. Belinsky's succession of philosophies suited the needs of an indigent writer in search of a message, but was alien to the spirit of objective philosophic thought. Belinsky, like Neverov and Bakunin, admired and loved an ideal which he saw embodied in Stankevich, but remained impervious to its influence.

And indeed it is clear that the intellectual personality of Stankevich —urbane, intensely civilized, expert in the languages of Western Europe, exacting in the study of philosophy, measured in judgment and clear in expression, at once Russian and profoundly cosmopolitan—left only the slightest trace on those who claimed to be his heirs. Much of what occurred after his departure from the intellectual life of the circle was alien and distasteful to him. We can confidently assert that the disorderly debate of the forties between "westernizers" and "Slavophiles" would have seemed pointless to Stankevich. In the diary he kept during his visit to Prague, he set down his impressions of the Czech Slavophiles, the linguist Šafařik and the poet Čekalovsky, who distressed him with their inane chauvinistic argument that "Slavs should not be studying German; rather, Germans should be studying the Slavic tongues." And before the "Slavophile-westernizer" controversy had even begun in Russia, Stankevich wrote the following anticipation of it in his diary:

Why are people so concerned about the "national character"? One should seek that which is human, and then a special personality will appear of its own accord. . . . One who has his own character will exhibit that character in all his actions; but it is possible to create a character—to educate oneself—only on general human principles. To invent or fabricate the character of a nation on the basis of ancient history and custom would simply mean the prolonging of that nation's infancy. Offer the nation general human [education], and see to it that she is able to absorb what she needs and does not have. That's the kind of national spirit to develop. But it's no good artificially to preserve ancient customs. (p. 754.)

Stankevich rejected the narrow concept of "national character" (*narodnost*) that runs like a thread through the long debate over Russia's role in history. Clarity, humanity, and European sophistication are evident in his brief comment. Of this legacy we find hardly any trace in Belinsky, or indeed in the work of Konstantin Aksakov, Apollon Grigoriev, Dostoevsky, or any of the great conservative ideologues of the nineteenth century.

# 7

# Letters to Granovsky

Another member of the Moscow circle who claimed to have been guided by the spirit of Stankevich was Timofei Granovsky, a professor at Moscow University whose lectures on history were an event of some importance during the forties and fifties. The epistolary exchange between these two men is interesting because of Stankevich's letters, which reveal many realistic details about his life in Berlin, and contain vivid characterizations of his mistress, Berta, as well as gay parodies of the philosophical seances held by the Berlin circle. Granovsky's letters, on the other hand, are rather flat, carefully phrased in either French or Russian, and slightly sentimental. But our picture of Stankevich would be incomplete without his letters to Granovsky.*

These letters, all of them written during the last four years of Stankevich's life, when he had become sure of his real interests, provide the fullest and most reliable portrait of his mind and personality at this time. One of these letters sets forth the history of his intellectual life, with a frank evaluation of its various "phases." Written in Berlin, this letter contains an invocation to "Berlin! . . . that German city on which each one of us has built his fondest hopes!" This reveals the attitude of Stankevich's circle toward that city which was felt to be the promised land of poetry and philosophy. As Stankevich presents it in this letter, his intellectual development has been a perilous passage between the Scylla of practical activity and the Charybdis of theoretical empiricism, from which voyage he has at last emerged

---

* Full publication data for all works referred to in this chapter will be found in the Bibliography.

into the serene waters of poetry and philosophy. At one time, he says, he had allowed himself to be influenced by shallow minds and then his own aims had been the shallow ones of social success and proper practical activity. In his decision to specialize in history he had not been following his own bent, but had been influenced by others, principally Neverov. Nadezhdin's lectures on esthetic theory, for all their inadequacy, gave him a feeling for the beautiful, and it was the work of Schelling—upon which he happened by accident—that showed him his own true path. Now he has an aim: "To find complete unity in the world of my knowledge. To understand each separate phenomenon and to see its connection with the life of the whole world, its necessity, and its role in the development of the single, unitary idea."

A practical interest in research and investigation he honors, but feels he does not have the kind of fanaticism required to dig out the facts in history or science—a one-sided, limited activity. Divine synthesis is what he requires. (There is a gap in his argument, since he doesn't specify what facts are to be generalized and synthesized, and how they are to be tested.) One should not study history simply as empirical science divorced from the "Idea," but history itself is to provide the concrete content, the imagery, wherein the "Idea" finds its illustration. Information is dead matter if it is unrelated to the questions which the mind asks. "Poetry and philosophy are the soul of existence."

The letter in which these statements occur provides a clear exposition of Stankevich's intellectual outlook and that of the generation to which he belonged. In offhand and unstudied phrases, Stankevich expresses their deep reverence for German idealism, and their rejection of empiricism (associated in their minds with French and English thought) along with all manner of scientific burrowing in the coarse immediacy of matter. Philosophy, as Stankevich was to say in the essay written just before his death, is a journey to the Absolute.

Stankevich's letters to Granovsky were literary exercises undertaken as a relaxation from the rigors of speculative thought. Nearly all the letters to Granovsky are jocular, chaffing, or satirical; for instance, this persiflage in the form of a philosophical discussion:

Child Timofei! What is Man? A bit of dirt. This definition is exact, if I am a man. Quiet! Quiet! I know you want to object, but I don't like flattery. . . .

We are in Dresden. "What emotions move thy soul, which is like to the sea?" you ask. Hm! Soul? What is the soul? *Reflexion in sich*. What is the sea? *Reflexion in Anderes*. The sun brought together certain atoms, for joy and grief, and this union of atoms Father Ivan [the priest who baptized him] named "the slave of God, Nikolai," and this Nikolai remained a slave of God, and by the Lord's mercy emerged alive from many sicknesses and misfortunes, and by His justice is not at all becoming a proper person, and by His inscrutable fate is dragged from Berlin to Dresden and from Dresden to Berlin. *Fiat voluntas tua,* says the slave of God, who picked up this Latin phrase in one of Walter Scott's novels. Apart from the ability to experience joy and sorrow, as well as the faculty of reflection, there is not within those atoms any force which calls itself "I myself." Life with its bad weather and clear skies . . . every miserable little town with its potato-selling women, every stinking side street in Dresden—all of this may boast of its preeminence over that creature, who, being raised to the degree of the general, is called the "Czar of Nature," and at the degree of the individual, Nikolai Vladimirovich Stankevich. What, briefly, is the sense of this lengthy tirade? But what do you want with sense, Timofei Granovsky? Sense is not hay nor oats—it isn't supplied in bundles. And anyway, if there's no sense in the text, why should there be any in the commentary? And if you think this is just the Foreword, you are mistaken. It's a voice from the other world.* (pp. 456–57.)

The following is a distracted but humorous complaint about the abstract constructs of the philosophers, which exist in the mind only:

In surrendering oneself, one finds himself—an axiom the truth of which could be doubted only by a shoeshine boy or a banker. But why, then, is this truth in the head only? The heart is empty, cold, and capricious just because it needs this truth. Why, then, does it not enter the heart? You know that when you are hungry and some soup is set before you (or hay, Timofei), you simply pour it and drink it. What's wrong with that?

After seeing you off I went to a restaurant, and taking my place at a table, I began in my grief to sip soup. . . . In the distance, a young French girl, by the immediacy of her being, introduced harmony into my soul. (p. 461.)

---

* Excerpts taken from the correspondence of Stankevich will be found in N. V. Stankevich, *Perepiska Nikolaya Vladimirovicha Stankevicha, 1830–1840,* red. i izd. Alekseya Stankevicha (Moscow, 1914), at the pages indicated in this text.

Annenkov understood these passages to mean that Stankevich, after years of painful immersion in German metaphysics, was now taking a saner and more realistic view of the world. Though Annenkov completely misses the light parody intended by Stankevich, it is no doubt true that during the Berlin period the element of humor, always a strong ingredient in Stankevich's spirit, exercised itself to good effect on the metaphysical preoccupation of the circle. This did not mean that Stankevich lost interest in philosophy but rather that he was developing a clearer and more realistic approach to it. The misty verbalization, sticky self-pity, and religious emotionalism occasionally found in the letters written while he was a student in Moscow do not appear in the letters of his Berlin period.

### Stankevich and Berta

During the Berlin period, Stankevich shed the habiliments of chastity which he had put on in his search for the ideal love. He was not the same young man who had written to Bakunin that "one should not know women." As a student in Berlin he did "know" at least one— a young woman named Berta, whose "uncle" claimed to be a "baron," and who lived with Stankevich as his mistress. His descriptions of Berta's flirtatious and fun-loving nature form an entertaining part of his correspondence with Granovsky. Like so much in the real life of Stankevich, Berta may have had a literary model. In her irresponsible but gaily affectionate nature, she bears a strong resemblance to Philina in Goethe's *Wilhelm Meister*.

When Stankevich wished to cancel a trip to Potsdam because of illness, Berta would have none of it. "If you are weak," she said, "then drink some wine or chocolate; but you must have the trip." She gave him some locks of her own hair in a golden frame inscribed "Berta." "How bourgeois and romantic!" was his comment. She made herself a new dress "as light as down feathers." She was a great consolation to Stankevich, for she refused to lament about his sickness or about anything else, and only told amusing stories. When she visited him on Good Friday, she said she felt something like a touch of compunction, but Stankevich reassured her, solemnly "taking the sin" on his own soul. Separated from her in Dresden, he wrote: "*O schwäches Herz*. How I'd love to see her." But he knew she was unfaithful. "If I were certain that there was in her even a crumb of real attachment to me, I would go back to Berlin. . . . But she's only a phantom. . . . Yet why expect anything else? I didn't love her, either." Finally the affair ended, though not until he had written her some foolish letters. "But our correspondence is now very infrequent," he wrote in February 1840. "She's beginning to understand, it seems, that it's better this way. . . . I've never answered her lamentations and so she's given them up. For the rest, it's just a matter of money. And that's unpleasant. . . . But I'm sad about my relationship with her: she's not all false—nor is she all true. I don't know just what my role was in her relations with that uncle. . . . But to the devil with her now. . . . I'll do whatever I can for her."[1]

Stankevich's infatuation with Berta, which Annenkov explains as a kind of spiritual relaxation after years of metaphysical effort, may actually have been a result of the exacerbated sexual urges that often accompany severe attacks of pulmonary tuberculosis. The affair blossomed at a time when Stankevich was acutely ill, and reports of Berta's charms alternate in his correspondence with alarmed accounts of severe coughing, and of blood issuing from the lungs.

Stankevich soon left Germany for Italy, and he was in Florence early in 1840. He then traveled to Rome, where Varvara Bakunin joined him. Thus it happened that his lighthearted affair with Berta was followed by a brief but very elevated love, the substance of which was passionately shared concern with the great unanswered questions of life and death.

# 8

# Stankevich as a Historical Figure

The doctrine that Stankevich was a saintly hero and a beneficent genius is, as we have seen, enshrined in the two works that deal directly with him and his circle—Annenkov's *Biography* and Herzen's *My Life and Thoughts*. It should be interesting and instructive to trace what we may now call the "legend" of Stankevich through later periods in the history of the Russian intelligentsia, for the treatment of that legend provides clues to the intellectual character of particular periods and particular historical writers.*

In 1855, one of the leaders of radical thought, N. V. Chernyshevsky, initiated the public discussion of literary and intellectual figures prominent in the thirties by publishing a series of essays entitled *Sketches of the Gogol Period in Russian Literature*. He gives principal attention to Belinsky's contributions to criticism and philosophy, but he also speaks of Stankevich as the "soul" of the Moscow circle, and credits him with having introduced the study of Hegel's philosophy in Moscow. Chernyshevsky is cautious, however. He admits that very little is definitely known about Stankevich, and suggests that it is high time a monograph was written "on this pure and noble episode in the history of Russian literature." Chernyshevsky, a materialist and positivist, the enemy of idealism and the romantic spirit, saw no reason to reject the idea that Stankevich was the "soul" and the "teacher" of his circle.

Annenkov's monograph was, in a sense, an answer to Chernyshev-

* Full publication data for all works referred to in this chapter will be found in the Bibliography.

sky's suggestion. Immediately upon the appearance of Annenkov's work, a highly skeptical review appeared in the *Library for Reading*. Its author, Ilya Lkhovsky, questioned Annenkov's thesis that Stankevich, though he had produced little, had been a powerful and salutary influence on Russian literature and intellectual life. Lkhovsky dwelt upon Stankevich's idleness, his distaste for the detail of scholarly investigation, his constant search for esthetic pleasure, his fantasy-prone escapism. Lkhovsky, a long-winded and laborious scholar, found Stankevitch essentially frivolous and his life quite unimportant. In fact, as a positive and practical man, Lkhovsky refused to attribute great influence to a young man who had no single concrete labor to his credit. The aristocratic, fanciful young dreamer and poet is temperamentally and socially alien to Lkhovsky, whose sympathies are clearly with those who must labor for the bread of fame. He is impatient at the apparently effortless ascendancy of Stankevich, who seems to him only an upper-class voluptuary brilliantly dabbling in the affairs of the mind. He asks for concrete, specific evidence of Stankevich's influence on Russian life and thought. In fact, he would introduce the criteria of common sense into the discussion. Lkhovsky reminds one inescapably of the sensible privy councillors, Latin teachers, and other philistines in E. T. A. Hoffmann's *The Golden Pot* who would burden Anselmus with reality and dispel for him his own world of mystery and imagination.

Lkhovsky's article was promptly and crushingly answered by one of the leading progressive critics of the day, N. A. Dobrolyubov. His long and detailed rebuttal of Lkhovsky is based on evidence, drawn from the letters published by Annenkov, that many of Belinsky's most important ideas were developed first in Stankevich's correspondence. Thus Dobrolyubov was the first to attempt a documentation in specific terms of the sweeping claims made for Stankevich by Herzen and Annenkov. His evidence is indeed impressive, and his argument has been acceptable, until Soviet times, even to leftist elements among the Russian intelligentsia. It is one of history's milder ironies that it should be Dobrolyubov, a rationalist, a realist, and a materialist, who found evidence to support the romantic legend propagated by Herzen and Annenkov. His essay as a whole seems intended to illustrate the problem of the individual in history, with particular reference to Stankevich. He takes the moderate position that individual personalities like Stankevich, though they cannot determine the course of history, do at times have an effect on particular but important events.He regards Stankevich as an important causative force in Russian intellectual history.

The authority of Chernyshevsky and Dobrolyubov, added to that of Herzen and Annenkov, was sufficient to maintain through several generations the notion that Stankevich was an important "influence." The belief remained firm that behind Belinsky and his followers there had been a purer essence, a "soul" who had guided and instructed them. Lkhovsky's doubts were to be raised again, however, and as time passed, the figure of Stankevich tended to become blurred, as historians necessarily gave attention to the voluminous published work of his supposed disciples. In the seventies, A. M. Skabichevsky produced the essays which eventually appeared under the title *Forty Years of Russian Criticism,* an obtuse and prejudiced book from the hand of a critic and cultural historian who had strong appeal for the radical reading public. For Skabichevsky, class, rank, and social status are significant, and Stankevich, as a son of landowners, is automatically suspect. Skabichevsky twists his evidence a bit in order to present Stankevich as a kind of pampered young nobleman along the lines of Fonvizin's Mitrofanushka, and compares him for idleness and sterility to Oblomov (also a member of the provincial nobility). Skabichevsky holds that the plebeian critic Belinsky was constitutionally incapable of succumbing to the "influence" of upper-class "otherworldliness" in the person of Stankevich, and that the former's hard ideological path, with its many windings, was simply a journey into the world of "reality." Skabichevsky's work is dull, bigoted, classconscious, and rather ignorant. Though he rejects Herzen's view of the circles, he slavishly follows Herzen's account of them. He portrays Stankevich as a useless aristocrat unfit for the nimbus he had worn. Skabichevsky, a forerunner of certain Soviet scholars of the Stalin period, gives expression in much of what he writes to the gathering mood of radicalism in the seventies and eighties.

On the other hand, A. N. Pypin, a serious scholar who contributed heavily to our knowledge of folk literature and medieval tales, was the first person to attempt a systematic study of Belinsky. There is a lengthy and detailed section on the circles in his book *Belinsky, His Biography and Correspondence,* which was written in the seventies. Pypin's researches indicate that because Belinsky's range of reading, acquaintance, and activity was very wide, his debt to Stankevich must be a specific and relatively modest one. He emphasizes the debt of both Belinsky and Stankevich to the lectures of Nadezhdin, a debt that Stankevich, at least, fully acknowledged in his lifetime. For Pypin, the important thing was to demonstrate that Belinsky, the subject of his lengthy biography, was an original thinker. His demonstration of this is not convincing, and in any case, Pypin does not deny that Stankevich was one of those who played a critically important role in Belinsky's development. To the reader who might want to know more about Stankevich he recommends—with great respect— the works of Herzen and Annenkov.

Toward the end of the nineteenth century, Ivan Ivanov produced his excellent *History of Russian Criticism,* a book that not only deals perceptively with literature and criticism, but touches upon ideas, philosophical systems, and the movement of thought. Ivanov recognizes Stankevich as a genuine philosopher, in the sense that he rejected the vulgar demand that philosophy have practical applications. He recognizes also that Belinsky was in tune with the dominant Russian tendency to make philosophy understandable to the reading public, and to draw upon it for social and political wisdom. Ivanov erroneously maintains that Stankevich was indifferent to practical life and practical concerns, and totally immersed in the contemplation of beauty and the search for truth. Though Ivanov does provide a stimulating and original critique, he did not fundamentally alter the conventional interpretation of the thirties and the circle.

Stankevich's love life was the subject of three scholarly investigations produced early in the present century. This emphasis on Stankevich's "erotic" experiences parallels the marked increase in attention to carnal affairs that was developing at about the same time in literature. This was the decade of Artsybashev's daring, though dull, sensationalism, of Gorky's romantic naturalism, and of Andreyev's and Kuprin's sexual "abysses." It is rather amusing to find the tone of the period palely reflected even in contemporary scholarly studies of the "divine" Stankevich.

The trend toward sexual interpretation was initiated at the turn of the century by Pavel N. Milyukov, the famous political figure and historian of ideas. In 1902, he published an intriguing if narrowly focused study of Stankevich and his friends under the title "Love Among the Idealists of the Thirties." Milyukov drew principally on Stankevich's letters to Neverov and Bakunin, feeling that they contained the clearest expression of the exalted view of love cultivated in the circle. He found the cause of the circle's romantic misadventures in the romantic philosophical notion that through love, man experiences his unity with the universal spirit. Milyukov's approach is modern and pragmatic: thoughts about love can hardly be justified if they tend to frustrate the deeds of love. But Stankevich, as Milyukov shows, subjected each of his love experiences to stern philosophical analysis, as a result of which the immediacy of love, and even its object, tended to vanish from his consciousness. Abstract idealism, Milyukov maintained, was the principal vice of all these young men. Stankevich to some degree fought free of it in Berlin, where he gave himself without "reflection" to the "real" love of his agreeable companion and easy paramour, Berta.

A. A. Kornilov's work on Bakunin, to which we have already referred, is a massive and truly magnificent tome which draws upon the Bakunin family archive in tracing the life of Mikhail Bakunin during the period of his association with Stankevich. It provides a wealth of detail on Stankevich's love life. Kornilov had at his disposal a mass of documentary material, most of it epistolary, and since he quotes from it generously and at length, the reading of his work is almost as good as a visit to the archive itself. Unfortunately, the work offers little more than documentation. Kornilov is scholarly, objective, deep in facts and footnotes, full of precious information, insatiable in his search for the last grain of historical evidence, and persistent in tracing even minor figures; but he lacks insight and eschews ideas,

A third study of Stankevich's amatory history, which also appeared in 1915, was N. Kashin's "Stankevich's Love Affairs," an essay that might have been written as a self-parody by an academic pedant. It has much in common with Kornilov's work: infinite patience, exacting self-discipline, and a passion for detail are brought to bear upon the problem of the chronology of each affair. Crumbs of evidence are collected and transformed into a full table of exact historical detail concerning the progress, week by week, of each amatory episode. It is all very weighty and impressive, and in some particulars Kashin is able to confute the opinions of earlier commentators; but the human subject of his investigation seems to move in a dimension that has nothing to do with Kashin's scholarly work. Indeed, the researcher almost loses sight of his subject, so absorbed is he in the niceties of documentation. Kashin's work is an extreme example of the excesses of the "biographical" school of criticism in the early twentieth century. However, the fact that massive efforts were devoted to a biography of Stankevich indicates that great importance was attached to him.

In 1915, P. V. Sakulin, a Marxist and a member of the sociological school of critics, published a brief but important essay entitled "The Idealism of N. V. Stankevich," in which he made a number of new and interesting points. A reference to Feuerbach in a letter Stankevich wrote in 1840 suggested to Sakulin that Stankevich was moving in the direction of materialism toward the end of his life, although the reference in the letter is, in fact, incidental and unemphatic, and is not supported by other evidence. Sakulin recognized that Stankevich had been religious even in his approach to philosophy, but saw in the young man's undogmatic tolerance of Catholic, Protestant, and unbeliever something akin to modern religious attitudes, and specifically to Tolstoy's "religion of love." In Sakulin's study, Stankevich emerges as a kind of Unitarian with transcendental leanings who is moving in the direction of materialism—perhaps even socialism.

Far removed from socialist theoreticians and pragmatic scholars was the philosopher M. O. Gershenzon, who wrote a lengthy study of Stankevich in 1904, which in 1908 was reprinted in Gershenzon's book *The History of Young Russia*. This work was regarded as important enough to be republished in 1923, even though Gershenzon's views on most matters were repugnant to the Soviet regime. Gershenzon was an idealist in philosophy, and, if the term be permitted, a subjectivist in his historical and biographical studies. His specialty was imaginative recreation of historical figures, and he has produced interesting portraits, each hovering on the borderline between history and fiction, of Pecherin, Chaadaev, Griboyedov, and Stankevich. He explicitly repudiated the search for social or political factors in intellectual history, and studied instead the growth of ideas in outstanding individuals. Gershenzon was deeply attracted to Stankevich, at least to those features of Stankevich's intellectual makeup with which he himself was in sensitive accord: his idealism, his religious attitude toward the world, and his concern with moral and philosophical questions. *A History of Young Russia* traces the awakening in Russia of idealistic philosophy; and Gershenzon hoped also to show that the esthetic and moral vision of Stankevich—and of Belinsky during the period when he was associated with Stankevich—had been a formative factor of prime importance in Russian life and thought. As Gershenzon himself said of the men of the thirties, "They set up the ideal of a life both joyful and beautiful. They were the first who raised that sun over the horizon of our social life, and since their day it has never set on the Russian intelligentsia. From that sun our literature has received its warmth and color."

This study gave new life to the Stankevich legend. To Gershenzon, the vision of that young idealist was the "dawn" that awakened the Russian imagination and contributed to Russian literature its elevated moral character. Gershenzon's phrasing is only an extreme formulation of a notion that has hovered for some time, unexamined and uncriticized, in the background of much Russian literary criticism. And Gershenzon's method is poorly suited to examine and criticize any idea. An unashamed subjectivism vitiates his work. By a process of solipsistic cerebration which he tries to validate by reference to random or arbitrary excerpts from historical documents, he succeeds in projecting upon the past what is essentially his own train of thought. We have observed a similar method in the work of earlier historians of this period. One interesting and pleasant result of this method is that in Gershenzon's book Stankevich's personality and ideas have definite form. But Gershenzon has not so much discovered the form as created it. Gershenzon inadvertently provides the key to his own method in the following comment on Stankevich: "In his eyes she [his beloved] has no autonomous importance; she is simply the raw material out of which his own spirit creates its ideal." So much for Gershenzon's "scholarship."

We turn now to the works of émigré scholars. Professor Dmitry Chizhevsky's outstanding work of scholarship, *Hegel in Russia* (1939), contains, along with a superflux of information on all other important figures of the era, an admiring account of Stankevich and his influence on the men of the thirties. Professor Chizhevsky recognizes in Stankevich a young man of the "conservative" stamp, an aristocratic, remote, apolitical philosopher for whom existing institutions were objects of reverence. It is obvious that Chizhevsky finds this type congenial, and naïvely assumes that other scholars will agree with him. He shares with Skabichevsky a palpable class prejudice, though Chizhevsky's animus is directed at plebeians rather than at aristocrats. Stankevich figures in Chizhevsky's book as a salutary and wise influence on his comrades, especially on the plebeian Belinsky. There can no longer be any doubt that he is mistaken when he says that "to a significant extent, Belinsky's Schellingianism can be explained by the influence of Stankevich," or that Belinsky as a literary critic "simply took over the literary sympathies of his intellectual leader." An unashamed snobbery, moreover, mars his scholarship when he comments—with some malice—on the awkwardness of Belinsky's phrasing, or on his (very infrequent) deviations from correct grammatical and spelling norms. Chizhevsky's flat statement that Stankevich "was never a romantic" is arbitrary and in conflict with fact. And he opens his discussion of Stankevich with an absentminded blunder. Herzen, he says, considered Stankevich "one of those idle people who accomplished nothing." This is, of course, the reverse of the truth; Chizhevsky simply missed the irony in Herzen's phrase. And yet, disfigured though it is by prejudice and errors of judgment, Chizhevsky's book is an indispensable storehouse of facts concerning an important intellectual movement. And because of the author's rich associative memory, the facts he sets down are often placed in interesting relationship to literary works and philosophical problems. His tendency when dealing with Stankevich is to maintain the legend of his "influence" and ascendancy among his comrades of the circle. Stankevich is elevated in order to diminish Belinsky, whom Chizhevsky regards as a dangerous democrat and a precursor of the Soviets.

The Soviet period, it is now well known, is distressingly poor not only in works on Stankevich and his circle but in the treatment of most literary, philosophical and historical problems. Soviet studies of Stankevich and his milieu are a kind of monstrous birth: they exhibit a formally correct and complete scholarly apparatus, with meticulous citation of sources both published and unpublished, but this is firmly tied to an unyielding dogmatism of interpretation. The Soviet investigator is unable to discover anything new when he burrows in books and manuscripts, because the accepted lines of historical interpretation have been laid down for him; and in the Soviet state, a markedly individual interpretation would seem in bad taste. Moreover, Soviet studies impress one as helplessly naïve, and this not so much because of their ready-made interpretations as because of the authors' conscientious and complete ignorance of any but the canonical books. Without doubt, Mashinsky's recent essays on Stankevich and his circle and his recent collection of the poetry produced by some of the circle's members mark a forward step in the Soviet investigation of Russian intellectual history; but neither Mashinsky's text, nor his footnotes, nor his bibliography betrays any acquaintance with works in German or French or English, or even with Russian works not in the accepted canon. The result of the self-imposed ignorance of Soviet scholars is heavyfooted documentation devoid of insight or ideas.

Nor is this due, in most cases, to the limitations of the scholars themselves. On the contrary, Mashinsky's work demonstrates, within the narrow area laid out for him, intelligence, complete control of the sources, and even the possibility of originality and style. But he, too, is obliged to torture the evidence in order to induce in himself the belief that Stankevich was, after all, an enemy of the Czarist social order. Mashinsky does insist however—and in this he disagrees with Nechaeva and Polyakov—that Stankevich was an important figure, almost on a level with Belinsky, in the development of Russian thought and literature. Belatedly, Soviet scholars have come to realize that their two unquestionable authorities, Chernyshevsky and Dobrolyubov, were strong partisans of Stankevich, and that Chernyshevsky himself urged the need for studying the Stankevich story, "that pure and noble episode in the history of Russian literature."

In tracing to the present time the role of Stankevich in Russian intellectual history, one is struck by the fact that, except for Lkhovsky, Skabichevsky, and certain writers of the Stalin period, no one has ever expressed serious doubt about the essential correctness of the portraits created by Annenkov and Herzen. There have been variations in emphasis and in the particular focus of interest, depending on the scholar and his times. Thus Sakulin develops a tenuous thread of evidence linking Stankevich with materialism, and Chizhevsky transforms him into an aristocratic intellectual snob. But the most interesting conclusion to be drawn from our survey of the literature on Stankevich is that the iconographic image created by his immediate followers has never—not even during the heyday of scientific rationalism—been successfully questioned. Voices raised against it have been directly answered by the leading spokesmen of each period. Dobrolyubov, as it seemed, crushingly refuted Lkhovsky; Skabichevsky's bigotry did not stand up before Pypin's scholarship; Nechaeva's partisan views are answered by implication in the work of Mashinsky. The noble image of Stankevich, freed from the contradictions and complexities of the real historical figure, has remained unchanged in the Russian consciousness.

# Conclusion: Who Was Stankevich?

A not infrequent outcome of investigation intended to reveal "the man behind the myth" is the discovery that myth is more interesting and more viable than reality. That is not true of the present investigation. The "real" Stankevich is stronger, more various, and more attractive than the sentimental icon preserved for posterity; but he had only a minimal effect on the intellectual life of his times and probably none at all on the development of the Russian intelligentsia or Russian literature.

How did it happen that this engaging young man, the center of the Moscow circle in the 1830's, was depicted by his biographers as a saintly hero and beneficent genius? The fact that this happened is beyond question: the reasons for it are complex, and lead us into speculations both literary and psychological. The qualities that endeared Stankevich to his friends do come through to the reader of his unexpurgated correspondence. His mind was unusually bright and clear. He could reduce complex metaphysical problems to simple terms, and he did help his friends to understand difficult passages in Kant and Hegel. Possessing intellectual power of a high order, he was gentle in exercising it, and this quality of gentleness and restraint was rare among his contemporaries, who were fond of dispute and prone to arrogance. Alone among his friends, Stankevich possessed a salutary sense of humor, which enabled him at times to produce fine parodies of ideas and systems that others treated with solemn respect. His qualities of mind and heart made him a not unlikely candidate for canonization. Add to all of this the fact that he wasted away of consumption, and suffered and died while preserving his "faith" in the Absolute, and the resultant image irresistibly invites iconographic treatment.

The Stankevich myth was the religious creation of an essentially unreligious movement. The real person, Nikolai Stankevich, with his unhappy love affairs, his Berlin mistress, and his urge toward chastity, with his sense of ribald fun, is far more interesting as a human being than the idealized image created by the Russian intelligentsia of the 1850's. It was as a holy image, however, that he served them so well. It was precisely their need for a higher sanction and a leader above reproach that led them to create, collectively, the mythic figure. The fact that he died young made it possible for him to stand as an inspiration to intellectuals of whatever camp: to the radicals Belinsky and Herzen as well as to the Slavophile Aksakov. This would probably have been impossible if he had ever accomplished anything or clearly defined himself. But because his great promise was neither thwarted nor realized, he seemed in retrospect to have been without limitations.

The poverty of literature and philosophy in Russia also aided in the creation of the Stankevich myth. Throughout this study we have seen evidence of the intellectual destitution of early nineteenth century Russia. Chaadaev's "Philosophical Letter" on the barrenness of Russian history, Belinsky's articles on the dearth of Russian literature, Stankevich's comment that he could find no one in Moscow competent to help him with the difficulties of Kant—all these things are evidence of the late development in Moscow of an intellectual culture.

The acute consciousness among Russian intellectuals of Russia's backwardness in philosophy and literature has often led them to search in earlier periods for important and original figures. Sometimes such figures could be found; sometimes they had to be created. At the end of the eighteenth century, for instance, there came to light *The Lay of the Host of Igor,* a twelfth-century epic the discovery of which argued that before the Tartar invasion, a literary culture of some sophistication had existed in Kievan Russia. The authenticity of the *Lay,* it is true, has been questioned; but it has, to all appearances, been successfully defended. In response to similar needs, a popularizer of secondhand snatches of "wisdom," Skovoroda, has sometimes been dignified as an original Russian philosophical mind of the eighteenth century. Perhaps analogous intellectual pressures worked to help create the figure of Stankevich as a center of vital intellectual activity whose beneficial influence worked unseen beneath the surface of Russian life during the dark days of Nicholas I.

The paradoxical and complex history of Stankevich's reputation among his intellectual posterity throws light on the nature of myth-making, and may help us to understand better the kind of human need that is satisfied by the creation of heroic personalities. In the first place, Stankevich (as is perhaps true of most other saintly figures) supplied each of his disciples with perfections not possessed by the disciple himself. Each of Stankevich's closest friends is an example of this. The tormented and rebellious Bakunin, who made use of philosophy as a weapon for the propagation of his own anarchistic views, remembered as the "finest period of his life" the winter he spent with Stankevich, a student of philosophy whose mind was pure of ulterior intention. Belinsky was extreme in his views, whether they happened to be reactionary or radical; but his human ideal was a young man of the severest intellectual restraint. Annenkov, placid and prosaic in his garrulous middle age, found in Stankevich the inspiration of youth and moral fervor. Neverov was a practical official with little imagination and less poetry, but he cherished the memory of Stankevich as a fanciful young poet. Herzen lived in permanent exile from his native land, but for him Stankevich represented the pledge of Russia's extraordinary future mission—the creation of a just social order.

The process is even more striking and strange when we observe the contrast between Stankevich and the intellectual milieu that later claimed him. The gentle and perspicacious philosopher, who was reluctant to take a position on any subject, had little enough in common with the noisy and dogmatic debaters whose strife fills the pages of Russian history.

In the enlightened and skeptical nineteenth century, the icon-making process had to stop short of fashioning a full saint, complete with miracles and apparitions, but nevertheless the need for saints was present and deeply felt, and at times the biographies of Stankevich have an overtly hagiographic ring.

There were many special images of Stankevich, fashioned according to the particular need of each man who knew him, but the one quality that stands out in the memory of all is his "disinterestedness." Stankevich helped others without thought of advantage for himself; he enjoyed art without making practical demands on it; he studied philosophy for the sake of pure knowledge; he loved (or tried to love) women for the spirit in them, and not for their flesh. He suffered all his life and died tragically. Indeed, his life seemed to his surviving friends to have been a continuous abnegation of self. It was for this reason that they revered his memory. They elevated him to sainthood, not because they had understood his moral or intellectual ideals but because they had loved him.

# Notes

Complete authors' names, titles, and publication data
are given in the Bibliography, pp. 141–45.

CHAPTER I

1. Tolstoi, L. N., *Polnoe sobranie sochinenii,* Vol. 60, letter to Countess A. A. Tolstoi, August 23, 1858.

2. On the journals of the period see I. I. Zamotin, "Ocherk istorii zhurnalistiki za pervuyu polovinu XIX veka," in Ovsyaniko-Kulikovsky, *Istoriya russkoi literatury XIX veka,* Vol. II, pp. 374–97. Gershenzon, in *Istoriya molodoi Rossii,* pp. 217–18, observes that in the thirties and forties intellectual life flourished in "groups" and "circles," whereas in his own generation, the tendency was rather centrifugal: each man worked and thought for himself. Gershenzon goes on to explain that in the earlier period, the public apparatus of intellectual life did not exist (e.g., newspapers, journals, schools, books), and so individuals sought support and sustenance in a circle of like-minded friends. For the thirties and forties see *Russkaya periodicheskaya pechat',* 1702–1894gg. (Moscow, 1959).

3. Kireevsky, *Polnoe sobranie sochinenii,* Vol. I, pp. 86–95. P. Chaadaev's "Philosophical Letter" appeared in *The Telescope,* No. 7, 1836.

4. Belinsky, *Polnoe sobranie sochinenii,* Vol. I, pp. 20–104. This edition will be referred to hereafter as *Belinsky.*

5. See M. Polyakov, "Studentcheskie gody Belinskogo," in *Literaturnoe nasledstvo,* No. 56. The material first published in this article, along with much additional information, is given in *Belinsky v Moskve,* by the same author.

6. The members of the circle thus assisted Belinsky in 1835, while he was editing *The Telescope.* See Chapter 5, p. 96.

7. N. V. Stankevich, "Neskol'ko mgnovenii iz zhizni Grafa Z.," *Teleskop,* No. 21, 1834, pp. 220–316.

8. Turgenev, *Sobranie sochinenii,* Vol. X, p. 300.

9. Setschkareff, *Schellings Einfluss.*

10. Gershenzon, *Istoriya molodoi Rossii,* p. 191.

11. *Belinsky,* Vol. II, pp. 552–53. F. M. Dostoevsky, *Sobranie sochinenii* (Moscow, 1956), Vol. X, p. 456.

CHAPTER 2

1. Stankevich, *Perepiska*, p. 321.

2. *Ibid.*, p. 2.

3. A selection of Stankevich's poems is to be found in Annenkov's *Stankevich* and in N. V. Stankevich, *Stikhotvoreniya*. A more recent and complete collection is found in *Poety kruzhka N. V. Stankevicha*, ed. S. I. Mashinsky (Moscow, 1964).

4. *Belinsky*, Vol. XII, p. 98.

5. A. Stankevich, *T. N. Granovsky*, Vol. I, p. 172.

6. Letter to Bakunin dated Sept. 8, 1840, in *Polnoe Sobranie sochinenii i pisem* (1961), Vol. I, p. 195.

7. N. Brodsky, "Ya. M. Neverov," pp. 73–136.

8. In a recently published rough draft of a note on Stankevich, Neverov recalled that Stankevich, after hearing of Belinsky's expulsion from the university for the writing of a play, expressed the wish to read the play and make the acquaintance of the author. Neverov's reminiscence is certainly misleading in the impression it gives of Stankevich. It is simply inaccurate to say, as some Soviet scholars still do, that Belinsky was expelled because of his play. See *Literaturnoe nasledstvo*, Vol. 56, pp. 100f, and Chapter 5, p. 85.

9. Neverov, "I. S. Turgenev," p. 419.

10. Mashinsky, "Stankevich i ego kruzhok," pp. 125–38.

11. Aksakov, *Vospominaniya studentchestva*, pp. 9–13.

12. *Literaturnoe nasledstvo*, No. 56, p. 103.

13. *Perepiska*, pp. 411, 414.

14. Goncharov, "Iz universitetskikh vospominanii."

15. Kostenetsky, "Vospominaniya," No. 1 (1887), pp. 99–117; No. 2 (1887), pp. 228–44.

16. *Ibid.*, No. 1 (1887), p. 101.

17. Nechaeva, *V. G. Belinsky. Uchenie v universitete i rabota v "Teleskope" i "Molve,"* p. 184.

18. *Literaturnoe nasledstvo*, No. 56, pp. 362–64.

19. Pirogov, "Posmertnye zapiski," p. 13.

20. Turgenev, *Sobranie sochinenii*, Vol. XI, pp. 229–36.

21. See Aksakov, *Vospominaniya studentchestva*, p. 10.

22. Oksman sees in Turgenev's *Andrei Kolosov* certain resemblances to the "real" Stankevich. He points out, in a note to Turgenev's "Zapiska," that an episode concerning a trip with Stankevich to Albano is reproduced in the story "Prizraki," and that one of Stankevich's romantic poems is used in the story "Neschastnaya."

CHAPTER 3

1. Herzen, *Byloe i dumy*, Vol. I, pp. 136, 471.

2. *Ibid.*, pp. 216, 473.

3. *Ibid.*, pp. 72–116.

4. *Ibid.*, pp. 284, 286. Italics Herzen's.

5. See Chapter 5.

6. A. Stankevich, *T. N. Granovsky*, Vol. II, p. 417.

7. Herzen, *Byloe i dumy*, p. 304.

8. For additional material on this biography, see Arkhangelsky, "Po povodu pervoi biografii N. V. Stankevicha," pp. 95ff. The manuscript is preserved in the State Historical Museum, *Fund 351, Khr. No. 64.* See also *Literaturnoe nasledstvo*, No. 56, p. 169.

9. Annenkov, "Nikolai Vladimirovich Stankevich," *Russkii vestnik*, No. 7 (1857), pp. 441–49, 695–738. Annenkov's biography was first published in book form in 1858, with an appendix containing part of Stankevich's correspondence together with poems, articles, and his one story.

10. *Perepiska*, p. 452.

### CHAPTER 4

1. In 1858, Annenkov decided against publishing certain parts of Stankevich's correspondence. This material was made public in 1914 by Stankevich's nephew, Alexei Stankevich. However, it is certain that Alexei omitted some letters and passages that he felt might tarnish the reputation of his uncle. For example, the ribald abuse of Belinsky to be found in *Perepiska*, p. 414, was softened in Alexei's version by the omission of several phrases, and one of Stankevich's letters concerning "the liberation of Varvara" was left out altogether, probably because it showed Stankevich in the dubious role of conspirator. The "Varvara" letter has been published in *Literaturnoe nasledstvo*, No. 55, p. 418.

2. See *Perepiska*, p. iv.

3. *Ibid.*, pp. 621, 261–62.

4. Many of Belinsky's lengthy missives have the appearance of "essays," and he so styles them. However, they have a quality of spontaneous untidiness that rules out the possibility that he intended them for eventual publication.

5. See Chapter 2, note 7.

6. *Perepiska*, p. iv.

7. Brodsky, *Ya. M. Neverov i ego avtobiografiya*, p. 112.

8. *Ibid.*, pp. 78ff.

9. From Neverov's unpublished correspondence, in the State Historical Museum, Moscow, *Fund No. 351: Khr. No. 57.*

10. *Perepiska*, p. 208.

11. Milyukov, *Iz istorii russkoi intelligentsii*, pp. 75ff.

12. Brodsky, *Ya. M. Neverov i ego avtobiografiya*, pp. 111–12.

13. *Perepiska*, p. 347.

14. *Ibid.*, p. 297.

15. *Ibid.*, p. 283.

### CHAPTER 5

1. In the passages that follow, the author is indebted to Carr's *Bakunin*, Steklov's *M. A. Bakunin*, Polonsky's *Materialy dlya biografii Bakunina*, Vol. I, and Kornilov's *Molodye gody Mikhaila Bakunina*.

2. See for instance, Carr, *Bakunin*, pp. 49–71.

3. Kornilov, *Mikhaila Bakunina*, p. 142.

4. See Chizhevsky, *Gegel' v Rossii*, pp. 106ff.

5. Carr, *Bakunin*, pp. 18, 19.

6. Kornilov, *Mikhaila Bakunina*, pp. 82–90.

7. Turgenev, in his physical description of Rudin in the novel of that name, drew a picture reminiscent of the young Bakunin. See also Belinsky's marvelous description in *Belinsky*, Vol. XI, p. 242.

8. There are generous quotations from these in Kornilov, *Mikhaila Bakunina*, pp. 130ff.

9. The Beyer family was important in the intellectual life of Moscow. The members of the Stankevich circle were regularly entertained there.

10. Kornilov, *Mikhaila Bakunina*, p. 131.

11. *Perepiska*, pp. 571–72; Kornilov, *Mikhaila Bakunina*, p. 135; Steklov, *M. A. Bakunin*, Vol. I, pp. 178–79.

12. Kornilov, *Mikhaila Bakunina*, p. 89.

13. Belinsky made much of this trait in his angry correspondence with Bakunin. *Belinsky*, Vol. XI, p. 245.

14. Polonsky, *Materialy dlya biografii Bakunina*, p. 31, says that Stankevich gave Bakunin the volume to read; but this is in no way borne out by the correspondence.

15. See Steklov, *M. A. Bakunin*, Vol. I, letters written by Bakunin in 1836 and 1837 to his sisters and to the Beyer family.

16. Perhaps the most extreme statement of "Fichtean exaltation" is to be found in *Belinsky*, Vol. XI, pp. 140–56. In this letter, Belinsky refers to "two works" of Fichte: *Über die Bestimmung des Gelehrten,* and *Die Anweisung zum seligen Leben*. Bakunin translated the first of these into Russian for *The Telescope,* No. 29, 1835.

17. Evidence for this point of view is to be found, in the main, in the correspondence of Bakunin during 1836 and 1837, as published in Steklov, *M. A. Bakunin*, Vol. I. See also Kornilov, *Mikhaila Bakunina*, pp. 136–70.

18. See below, Chapter 5.

19. Belinsky's correspondence demonstrates that his knowledge of Hegel came to him from one other person: Katkov. Katkov introduced him to the esthetics of Hegel. See *Belinsky*, Vol. XI, p. 387.

20. Carr's biography, excellent though it is in its treatment of other periods in Bakunin's life, does less than justice to the Stankevich circle. Carr tells of the concerns of this group from the viewpoint of a sensible, older man, who is positive and realistic. His brief generalizations on the romantic philosophy are not intended to explain it but rather to characterize and dispose of such nonsense.

21. As Milyukov points out in *Iz istorii russkoi intelligentsii,* p. 75.

22. Kornilov, *Mikhaila Bakunina*, p. 95.

23. *Ibid.,* p. 296. The various "loves" of Stankevich are treated with meticulous scholarly detachment in Kashin's "Romany N. V. Stankevicha," *Sovremennyi mir,* No. 8, 1915, pp. 1–41, an article in which there is no trace of conscious irony.

24. See Kashin, "Romany N. V. Stankevicha," pp. 28–29, and Kornilov, *Mikhaila Bakunina*, p. 303.

25. See the copious quotations from Stankevich's letters in Kornilov.

26. Kashin makes it perfectly clear that this letter, though it is the earliest preserved, cannot have been the first in the correspondence.

27. Stankevich repeatedly implored Bakunin not to read his letters about Liuba to family and friends. Kornilov, *Mikhaila Bakunina*, p. 301.

28. Kornilov, *Mikhaila Bakunina*, p. 298.

29. *Ibid.*, p. 305.

30. *Ibid.*, p. 303.

31. *Ibid.*, p. 371.

32. L. N. Maikov, "Vospominaniya I. S. Turgeneva o N. V. Stankeviche," *Vestnik Evropy*, January 1899, pp. 5–19. Maikov quotes a letter from Stankevich to Turgenev dated June 11, 1840, and written in Florence, in which this statement occurs (p. 16).

33. Kornilov, *Mikhaila Bakunina*, p. 308.

34. *Ibid.*, p. 648.

35. *Ibid.*, pp. 334ff.

36. *Ibid.*, p. 335.

37. *Ibid.*, p. 80.

38. Kornilov doubts this explanation and offers one of his own that is much less plausible. There is no reason to question the evidence of the letters of Bakunin and Stankevich (*Perepiska*, p. 523). Varvara herself never contradicted it, and complete self-immolation was quite consonant with her character.

39. See Carr, *Bakunin*, pp. 49–59.

40. Kornilov, *Mikhaila Bakunina*, p. 667.

## CHAPTER 6

1. *Belinsky*, Vol. XII, p. 107.

2. Nechaeva, *V. G. Belinsky; nachalo zhiznennogo*, p. 208.

3. *Belinsky*, Vol. XI, p. 19.

4. Oksman, *Letopis*, pp. 26ff. A number of letters home are quoted here.

5. *Ibid.*, pp. 32, 47.

6. See Nechaeva, *V. G. Belinsky; uchenie*, pp. 159ff, for a full statement of all facts and particulars.

7. Oksman, *Letopis*, p. 37.

8. *Belinsky*, Vol. XI, p. 49.

9. Oksman, *Letopis*, pp. 38, 40, 41.

10. *Ibid.*, p. 116.

11. *Belinsky*, Vol. XI, pp. 103, 104.

12. *Literaturnoe nasledstvo*, No. 56, p. 100.

13. *Belinsky*, Vol. XI, pp. 193, 206, 208, 229, 247, 293, 332, 487, 547, 554.

14. *Ibid.*, Vol. XII, p. 98.

15. Dobrolyubov, *Sochineniya*, Vol. I, pp. 791–815.

16. *Belinsky*, Vol. XI, p. 272.

17. The article in question was "Literaturnye opaseniya na budushchii god," in *Vestnik Evropy*, Nos. 21 and 22, 1828.

18. Nechaeva, *V. G. Belinsky; uchenie,* pp. 190–203, 199.

19. *Belinsky*, Vol. I, pp. 30–31.

20. Oksman, *Letopis,* p. 119.

21. *Belinsky*, Vol. XI, p. 202.

22. *Ibid.,* p. 35.

23. *Ibid.,* p. 558.

24. Werder, *Gedichte,* pp. 68–69.

25. Annenkov, "Biografiya," pp. 389–90.

26. *Belinsky*, Vol. XI, p. 329.

27. These are very well brought out by Nechaeva, *V. G. Belinsky; uchenie, passim.*

28. *Belinsky*, Vol. XI, p. 173.

29. *Ibid.,* letter to Bakunin, October 12–24, 1838.

30. For instance, in Belinsky's own article "Literary Musings."

31. Brodsky, *Belinsky i ego korrespondenty* (letters to N. M. Satin).

32. *Belinsky*, Vol. XI, p. 187.

33. *Ibid.,* p. 386.

34. *Ibid.,* pp. 386, 387–88.

35. Oksman, *Letopis,* pp. 228, 229.

36. *Ibid.,* p. 265.

37. *Belinsky*, Vol. XII, pp. 22, 23.

38. Oksman, *Letopis,* pp. 309, 313, 326, 339.

39. As translated in Guerney, *A Treasury of Russian Literature,* p. 243.

40. As Chizhevsky points out in *Gegel' v Rossii.*

CHAPTER 7

1. N. V. Stankevich, *Perepiska Nikolaya Vladimirovicha Stankevicha, 1830–1840,* red. i izd. Alekseya Stankevicha (Moscow, 1914), pp. 451, 454, 456, 467, 470, 475–77, 485.

# Bibliography

Aksakov, K. S. Vospominaniya studentchestva, 1832–1835 godov. St. Petersburg, 1911.

Annenkov, P. V. "Nikolai Vladimirovich Stankevich, biograficheskii ocherk," *Russki vestnik,* No. 7 (1857), 441–49, 695–738.

———. Literaturnye vospominaniya. St. Petersburg, 1909. Reissued Leningrad, 1960.

———. Nikolai Vladimirovich Stankevich; perepiska ego i biografiya. Moscow, 1858.

———. P. V. Annenkov i ego druzya: Literaturnye vospominaniya i perepiska 1835–1885. Moscow, 1892.

Arkhangelsky, K. P. "Po povodu pervoi biografii N. V. Stankevicha," *Trudy Voronezhskogo gosudarstvennogo universiteta,* III (1926), 95ff.

———. "N. V. Stankevich," *Izv. Sev.-Kavkaz. universiteta,* 1930, I(18), 92–153.

Aronson, M., and S. Reiser. Literaturnye kruzhki i salony (redaktsiya i predislovie B. M. Eikhenbauma). Leningrad, 1929.

Bakunin, M. A. Sobranie sochinenii i pisem (1828–1876). Pod redaktsiei i s primechaniyami Yu. M. Steklova. 4 vols. Moscow, 1934.

Barsukov, N. Zhizn i trudy Pogodina. St. Petersburg, 1888–1906.

Belinsky, V. G. Polnoe sobranie sochinenii. Moscow, 1953–1959.

Berezina, V. G. "Belinsky i Bakunin v 1830-ye gody," *Uchënie zapiski Leningradskogo ordena Lenina universiteta imeni A. A. Zhdanova,* 1952, No. 158, Vyp. 17, 34–86.

Berlin, Isaiah. "A Marvellous Decade," *Encounter,* Nos. 21, 26, 27 (1955).

Billig, J. Der Zusammenbruch des Idealismus bei den russischen Romantikern. Berlin, 1930.

Biograficheksy slovar' professorov i prepodavatelei Moskovskogo universiteta. Moscow, 1855.

Brodsky, N. L. Literaturnye salony i kruzhki, pervaya polovina XIX veka. Moscow, 1930.

———. "Poety kruzhka Stankevicha," Izvestiya otdeleniya russkogo yazyka i slovestnosti Imperatorskoi Akademii Nauk, Vol. XVII, No. 4 (Moscow, 1912), 1–70.

———. "Poeziya Stankevicha," *Vestnik vospitaniya,* March 1914, 1–6.

———. "Premukhinskii roman v zhizni i tvorchestve Turgeneva," Dokumenty po istorii literatury i obshchestvennosti. (Tsentrarkhiv, Vyp. 2.) Moscow, 1923.

———. "Ya. M. Neverov i ego avtobiografiya," *Vestnik vospitaniya,* No. 6 (1915), 73–136.

Brodsky, N. L., ed. Belinsky i ego korrespondenty. Sbornik Otdela rukopisei Gosudarstvennoi Publichnoi Biblioteki SSSR imeni V. I. Lenina. Moscow, 1948.

Carr, E. H. Bakunin. London, 1937.

Chernyshevsky, M. N. Ocherki gogolevskogo perioda russkoi literatury. St. Petersburg, 1893. First appeared in *Sovremennik,* 1855–1856.

Chizhevsky, D. I. Gegel v Rossii. Paris, 1939.

Dobrolyubov, N. A. Pervoe polnoe sobranie sochinenii. M. Lemke, ed. 4 vols. St. Petersburg, 1911.

Dostoevsky, F. M. Sobranie sochinenii. Vol. X. Moscow, 1956.

Elsberg, Ya. A. I. Gertsen, zhizn i tvorchestvo. 2nd ed. Moscow, 1951.

Florovsky, J. "Iskaniya molodogo Gertzena," *Sovremennye zapiski,* XI (1921), 338.

———. Puti russkogo bogosloviya. Paris, 1937.

Galich, Aleksandr. Istoriya filosofskikh sistem po inostrannym rukovodstvam sostavlennaya i izdannaya. . . . St. Petersburg, 1818.

———. Kartina cheloveka. St. Petersburg, 1834.

———. Opyt istorii filosofii. St. Petersburg, 1819.

Gershenzon, M. O. Istoriya molodoi Rossii. Moscow, 1923.

———, ed. P. Ya. Chaadaev, sochineniya i pisma. 2 vols. Moscow, 1913.

Goncharov, Ivan. "Iz universitetskikh vospominanii," *Vestnik evropy,* April 1887, 489–517.

Granjard, Henri. Ivan Tourguenev et les courants politiques et sociaux de son temps. Paris, 1954.

Guerney, B. G. A Treasury of Russian Literature. New York, 1943.

Hare, Richard. Portraits of Russian Personalities between Reform and Revolution. London, 1959.

Haumant, Emile. La culture française en Russie (1700–1900). 2nd ed. Paris, 1913.

Herzen, A. I. Byloe i dumy. 2 vols. Minsk, 1959.

———. Sobranie sochinenii v 30-ti tomakh. Moscow, 1954–61.

Ivanov, Ivan. Istoriya russkoi kritiki. 2 vols. St. Petersburg, 1900.

Ivanov-Razumnik, R. V. "Obshchestvennoe i umstvennoe techenie 30-x godov i ikh otrazhenie v literature," in Ovsyaniko-Kulikovsky, Istoriya russkoi literatury XIX v., I, 247ff.

Jarmerstedt, V. "Mirosozertsanie kruzhka Stankevicha i poeziya Koltsova," *Voprosy filosofii i psikhologii,* No. 5 (1894).

Kashin, N. "Romany N. Stankevicha," *Sovremennyi mir,* Nos. 7–8 (1915), 1–41.

Kireevsky, Ivan. Polnoe sobranie sochinenii. 2 vols. M. Gershenzon, ed. Moscow, 1911.

Kleman, M. Vissarion Grigorievich Belinskii v vospominaniakh sovremennikov. Leningrad, 1921.

Koltsov, A. V. Polnoe sobranie sochinenii. A. I. Lyashchenko, ed. 2nd ed. St. Petersburg, 1909.

Kornilov, A. Gody stranstvii M. Bakunina. Moscow, 1925.

——. Molodye gody Mikhaila Bakunina; iz istorii russkogo romantizma. Moscow, 1915.

Kostenetsky, Ya. I. "Vospominaniya iz moei studentcheskoi zhizni," *Russkii arkhiv*, No. 1 (1887), 99–117; No. 2 (1887), 228–44.

Kostka, Edmund. "At the Roots of Russian Westernism: N. V. Stankevich and His Circle," *Slavic and East European Studies*, VI, 158–76.

Koyré, Alexandre. Etudes sur la pensée philosophique en Russie. Paris, 1949.

——. La philosophie et le problème national en Russie au début du XIXe siècle. Paris, 1929.

Kozmin, N. K. "N. A. Polevoi, kak vyrazitel literaturnogo napravleniya sovremennoi emu epokhi," *Zapiski Istoriko-filologicheskogo fakulteta. Imp. Petersburgskogo Universiteta*. St. Petersburg, 1903.

——. Nikolai Ivanovich Nadezhdin: zhizn i nauchno-literaturnaya deyatelnost 1804–1836. St. Petersburg, 1912.

Labry, R. Alexandre Ivanovich Herzen. Paris, 1928.

——. Herzen et Proudhon. Paris, 1928.

Lampert, E. Studies in Rebellion. New York, 1957.

Lannes, Ferdinand. "Coup d'oeil sur l'histoire de la philosophie en Russie," *Revue philosophique*, XXXII (1891), 17–51.

——. "Le mouvement philosophique en Russie," *Revue philosophique*, XXXIV (1892), 561–89.

Lemke, M. K. Nikolaevskie zhandarmy i literatura, 1826–1855 gg. St. Petersburg, 1909.

——, ed. Polnoe sobranie sochinenii i pisem A. I. Gertsena. Vols. 1–22. Moscow, 1919–1925.

*Literaturnoe nasledstvo*, Nos. 22–24 (Moscow, 1935), Nos. 55–57 (Moscow, 1948–1951).

Lkhovsky, I. "Po povodu biografii Stankevicha," *Biblioteka dlya chteniya*, No. 3 (1858).

Maikov, L. N. "Vospominaniya I. S. Turgeneva o N. V. Stankeviche," *Vestnik evropy*, January 1899, 5–19.

Malia, Martin. Alexander Herzen and the Birth of Russian Socialism. Cambridge, 1961.

Masaryk, Thomas G. The Spirit of Russia. Studies in History, Literature, and Philosophy. Translated from the German original by E. and C. Paul. 2 vols. London, 1919.

Mashinsky, S. I. Poety kruzhka N. V. Stankevicha. Moscow, 1964.

——. "Stankevich i ego kruzhok," *Voprosy literatury*, No. 5 (1964).

Milyukov, P. Glavnye techeniya russkoi istoricheskoi mysli. 3rd ed. St. Petersburg, 1913.

——. Iz istorii russkoi intelligentsii (sbornik statei). St. Petersburg, 1902.

Mordovchenko, N. Belinsky i russkaya literatura ego vremeni. Moscow, 1950.
——. "Teleskop," in *Literaturnaya entsiklopediya,* Vol. XI.
Nadezhdin, Nikolai I. "Avtobiografiya," *Russkii vestnik,* No. 5 (1856).
——. "Neobkhodimost, znachenie, i sila esteticheskogo obrazovaniya," *Teleskop,* No. 3 (1831), 131–54.
Nechaeva, V. S. V. G. Belinsky; nachalo zhiznennogo puti i literaturnoi deyatelnosti. Moscow, 1949.
——. V. G. Belinsky; uchenie v universitete i rabota v "Teleskope" i "Molve." Moscow, 1954.
Nelidov, F. F. Zapadniki 40-x godov. Moscow, 1910.
Neverov, Ya. N. "I. S. Turgenev v vospominaniyakh Neverova," *Russkaya starina,* No. 11 (1883).
——. "Stranitsa iz istorii krepostnogo prava," *Russkaya starina,* December, 1883, 429–46.
Oksman, Yulyan. Letopis zhizni i tvorchestva Belinskogo. Moscow, 1958.
Ovsyaniko-Kulikovsky, D. N. Istoriya russkoi intelligentsii; itogi russkoi khudozhestvennoi literatury XIX veka. Moscow, 1906–1907.
Panaev, I. Literaturnye vospominaniya. R. V. Ivanov-Razumnik, ed. Leningrad, 1928.
Pirogov, N. I. "Posmertnye zapiski," *Russkaya starina,* No. 1 (1885).
Polonsky, V. A. Bakunin. Moscow, 1922.
——. Materialy dlya biografii Bakunina. 3 vols. Moscow, 1923–1933.
Polyakov, M. Ya. Belinsky v Moskve, 1829–1839. Moscow, 1948.
——. Vissarion Belinsky. Lichnost-idei-epokha. Moscow, 1960.
Pypin, A. N. Belinsky, ego zhizn i perepiska. 2nd ed. St. Petersburg, 1908.
——. Kharakteristika literaturnykh mnenii. St. Petersburg, 1873.
Quénet, Charles. Tchaadaeff et ses lettres philosophiques. Paris, 1931.
Reztsova, M. V. Nikolai Vladimirovich Stankevich. (Iz istorii russkoi mysli). Unpublished dissertation, defended June 4, 1945, at Moscow University.
Russkaya periodicheskaya pechat, 1702–1894 gg. Moscow, 1959.
Sakulin, P. "Idealizm N. V. Stankevicha," *Vestnik evropy,* February 1915, 246–64.
Satin, N. M. "Iz vospominanii N. M. Satina," *Pochin* (1895), 240.
Setschkareff, Wsewolod. Schellings Einfluss in der russischen Literatur der 20er und 30er Jahre des XIX Jahrhunderts. Berlin, 1939.
Shpet, G. G. Filosofskoe mirovozzrenie Gertsena. Petrograd, 1921.
——. Ocherk razvitiya russkoi filosofii. Petrograd, 1922.
Sidorov, N. I. "N. V. Stankevich (k stoletiyu so dnya rozhdeniya)," *Golos minuvshego,* No. 9 (1913), 1–7.
Skabichevsky, A. M. Sochineniya. 2 vols. St. Petersburg, 1903.
Stankevich, A., ed. T. N. Granovsky i ego perepiska. 2 vols. Moscow, 1897.
Stankevich, N. V. "Neskolko mgnovenii iz zhizni Grafa Z," *Teleskop,* No. 21 (1834), 220–316.
——. Perepiska Nikolaya Vladimirovicha Stankevicha, 1830–1840. A. Stankevich, ed. Moscow, 1914.

———. Stikhotvoreniya, Tragediya, Proza. A. Stankevich, ed. Moscow, 1890.

Steklov, Y. M. M. A. Bakunin, Sobranie sochinenii i pisem. 4 vols. Moscow, 1934–1936.

Tolstoi, L. N. Polnoe sobranie sochinenii. Vol. LX. Moscow, 1949. (Letter to Countess A. A. Tolstoi, August 23, 1858.)

Turgenev, I. S. "Odno iz rannikh pisem I. S. Turgeneva," *Russkaya mysl*, No. 12 (1912), 141–46.

———. Pervoe sobranie pisem, 1840–1883. St. Petersburg, 1884.

———. Polnoe sobranie sochinenii i pisem. 28 vols. Moscow, 1960.

———. Sobranie sochinenii v 12-i tomakh. Moscow, 1956.

Vellansky, D. M. Biologicheskoe issledovanie prirody v tvoryashchem i tvorimom yeyo kachestve. St. Petersburg, 1812.

Vvedensky, Aleksandr. "Sudby filosofii v Rossii," *Voprosy filosofii i psikhologii* (March–April 1898), 314–54.

Werder, Karl. Gedichte. Berlin, 1895.

Zamotin, I. I. "Ocherk istorii zhurnalistiki za pervuyu polovinu XIX veka," Ovsyaniko-Kulikovsky, in *Istoriya russkoi literatury* II, 374–97.

Zenkovsky, V. V. A History of Russian Philosophy. Translated by George L. Kline. 2 vols. London, 1953.

# Index